The Hastings Tower at Ashby-de-la-Zouch

THE CASTLES OF
THE EAST MIDLANDS

Mike Salter

FOLLY PUBLICATIONS

ACKNOWLEDGEMENTS

Most of the photographs in this book were taken by the author, and a number of old postcards from his collection have also been reproduced. The author also drew the plans and the map. Plans are drawn to common scales of 1:400 for keeps, towers and gatehouses, 1:800 for courtyard buildings, and 1:4000 and 1:10000 for site plans of large buildings and earthworks. Thanks to Anthony Morris for use of the postcard of Grimsthorpe and to Mike Osborne for Lincolnshire material and photographs of Bolingbroke, Hussey, Rochford, Somerton, South Kyme and Tower on the Moor. Helen Thomas took the close up picture of the keep at Peveril and drove on several fieldwork trips, when her brother James Randle provided accommodation.

AUTHOR'S NOTES

This series of books (see full list inside back cover) are intended as portable field guides giving as much information and illustrative material as possible in volumes of modest size, weight and price. As a whole the series gives a lot of information on lesser known castle sites about which little information has tended to appear in print. The aim in the castle books has been to mention, where the information is known to the author, owners or custodians of buildings who erected or altered parts of them, and those who were the first or last to hold an estate, an important office, or a title. Those in occupation at the time of dramatic events such as sieges or royal visits are also often named. Other owners and occupants whose lives had little effect on the condition of the buildings are not generally mentioned, nor are most 19th or 20th century events, unless particularly dramatic, nor ghost stories or legends. In keeping with the aims of all the castle books in this series work at Belvoir, Drayton and Rockingham of the 1660s and later is not illustrated or described in detail.

The books are intended to be used in conjunction with the Ordnance Survey 1:50,000 maps. Grid references are given in the gazetteers together with a coding system indicating which buildings can be visited or easily seen by the public which is explained on page 13. Generally speaking, maps will be required to find most of the lesser known sites, many of which are not regularly open to the public.

Measurements given in the text and scales on the plans are given in metres, the unit used by the author for all measurements taken on site. Although the buildings were designed using feet and inches the metric scales are much easier to use and are now standard amongst those studying historic buildings and ancient sites. For those who feel a need to make a conversion 3 metres is almost 10 feet. Unless specifically mentioned as otherwise all dimensions are external at or near ground level, but above the plinth if there is one. On plans the original work is shown black, post-1800 work is stippled, and alterations and additions of intermediate periods are hatched.

ABOUT THE AUTHOR

Mike Salter is 48 and has been a professional writer and publisher since he went on the Government Enterprise Allowance Scheme for unemployed people in 1988. He is particularly interested in the planning and layout of medieval buildings and has a huge collection of plans of castles and churches he has measured during tours (mostly by bicycle and motorcycle) throughout all parts of the British Isles since 1968. Wolverhampton born and bred, Mike now lives in an old cottage beside the Malvern Hills. His other interests include walking, maps, railways, board games, morris and folk dancing, and playing percussion instruments.

First published July 2002. Copyright Mike Salter 2002.
Folly Publications, Folly Cottage, 151 West Malvern Rd, Malvern, Worcs WR14 4AY
Printed by Aspect Design, 89 Newtown Rd, Malvern, Worcs WR14 2PD

Bolingbroke Castle

CONTENTS

A map of sites described appears inside the front cover.

INTRODUCTION

The story of castles in the East Midlands begins with the invasion by William, Duke of Normandy in 1066. During his twenty year reign as king of England William founded many castles, including those of Leicester, Lincoln, Nottingham, Rockingham, and possibly Oakham, which are described in this book. William gave estates to his chief followers in return for specified periods of military service, and the new lords gave units of land called manors to their knights, also in return for military service, which included garrison duty either in the lords' own castles or in those of the king, for which the lords were obliged to find knights to man them. This system was known as feudalism and was an innovation in England. The thin veneer of landowning and French-speaking Normans thus consolidated their fragile hold over the Saxon populace by constructing castles serving as residences, strongholds, and as symbols of rank. The Romans, Saxons and Danes all built forts and defended settlements as at Leicester and Lincoln, but the Normans introduced the idea of powerful individuals erecting fortresses to serve as their private residences and as the administrative centres of groups of manors. The Domesday Book commissioned by King William I in 1086 to record who was holding what land, and what it was considered to be worth, records (or implies) the existence of several of the castles described in this book, especially the royal castles in the county towns.

Castles built in the late 11th century often had a high mound raised from material taken out of the surrounding ditch, the top of which would be the lord's residence in the form of a two or three storey timber-framed tower surrounded by a palisade. The mound summit would be reached by a ramp up from a forecourt or bailey in which lay a range of stores, workshops, a hall and other apartments, and a chapel, all originally built of wood. Sometimes the mound took an alternative form known to modern writers as a ringwork, with a high rampart surrounding the lord's house, and the greater castles usually had an additional outer bailey beyond the main entrance. Castles of these types continued to be built for over a century after the Norman Conquest and can only be precisely dated when there is either a reliable historical record of their foundation or good archeological evidence, both of which are lacking for the majority of the many earthwork sites described in this book. The most impressive castles were the headquarters of great lords, but there were many smaller castles built by their followers. The basic design of these earthwork castles varied according to the terrain and the resources available, and in any case most of them were subject to additions and alterations over the years. Excavations have found instances of mottes being levelled, absorbed in a bailey rampart, or even added on later. Baileys and other outworks were omitted or duplicated and made whatever size and shape local circumstances dictated. Natural landscape features were used where possible, hillocks and spurs being shaped and heightened into steep-sided and level-topped mottes, whilst many castles on low ground were protected by wet moats filled from an adjacent stream or river.

The motte at Fotheringhay

East wall and Observatory Tower at Lincoln

For the first two generations after the Norman invasion of 1066 masons were in short supply compared with carpenters and labourers, partly because the Saxons mostly erected buildings of wood, except for the most important churches. Buildings of mortared stone took several years of comparatively peaceful conditions to construct. Fortifications would have been vulnerable to attack during the long periods when foundations were being laid, so structures raised quickly on timber posts and earth ramparts were seen as an easier option when defences were required in a hurry. Timber buildings were vulnerable to accidental or deliberate destruction by fire and eventually rotted away when in constant contact with damp soil. Although structures of wood remained an important element in the defences of most castles throughout the medieval period, at important castle the bailey palisade and the chief buildings within it would eventually be replaced by structures of mortared stone.

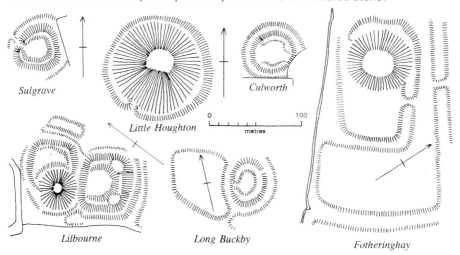

Plans of Norman castle earthworks in Northamptonshire

Few castles had stone buildings before the end of the 11th century, but at Peveril the north curtain wall closing off the only side not protected by cliffs may be as early as the 1070s. The Saxon motif of herringbone masonry appears here and in the west wall of the same castle and in parts of the curtain wall at Lincoln, both probably built early in Henry I's reign (1100-35). In the 1130s Bishop Alexander of Lincoln erected stone castles with quadrangular courtyards with square corner towers at Newark and Sleaford. Very little remains at Sleaford but Newark still has a one lofty corner tower and a very fine gatehouse. Probably of the same period was the huge keep at Duffield, of which only footings remain. Above dark basement rooms it contained on each level a hall and chamber side by side, a pattern set by the White Tower at London begun c1078. Lincoln has an unusually well preserved example of a shell keep, or a ring wall replacing a palisade on a motte summit, against which were once lean-to buildings. This keep may be of c1130-50, but could be as late as the 1170s. There were once similar keeps on the now-lowered motte summits of two other royal castles at Leicester and Rockingham, and another on a destroyed mound at Stamford.

The only Norman tower keep still standing high in the East Midlands is a small one built at Peveril in the 1170s by Henry II. It contained a single living room over a cellar. Henry probably also built the lost similar towers at Bolsover and at Nottingham, where he also built the curtain walls of the upper and middle baileys, with a huge hall in the latter, none of which has survived. The Lincolnshire castles of Bourne is also said to have had a tower keep. Little remains of slightly later keep at Horston in Derbyshire. Rare survivals are the little-altered aisled hall of c1175 at Oakham and the hall and chamber of 1200 raised over an undercroft within a moated platform at Boothby Pagnell. Parts of a much altered aisle hall of c1150 with arcades of timber instead of stone remain at Leicester. Another 12th century aisled hall at Stamford is known only from excavations and little remains of another hall at Peveril. The circuits of curtain walls at Bytham in Lincolnshire and Laxton in Nottinghamshire, both now reduced to buried footings amidst impressive earthworks, existed by the end of the 12th century, as did the vanished walls of Northampton, the standing but entirely refaced walls at Bolsover, and a curtain found by excavation at Wingfield.

The keep at Peveril Castle

North curtain wall at Peveril Castle

Earthworks at Castle Bytham

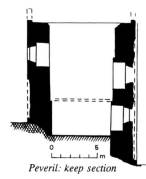

Peveril: keep section

The castle built by King John at Sauvey in Leicestershire in 1211 had a walled inner bailey and a palisaded outer bailey protecting the only side not enclosed by a lake. The Earl of Chester's Lincolnshire seat at Bolingbroke was of an advanced design, being a wet moated and thickly walled hexagon with huge D-shaped towers at five corners and a gatehouse flanked by two U-shaped towers at the sixth corner. The lower parts of most of it still remain. The gateway is the earliest in the East Midlands to have a groove for a portcullis. Just the footings of two round towers remain of a more modest castle of this type not far away at Tattershall. The curtain walls around large roughly rectangular baileys at Northampton and Oakham also had a series of round towers. Traces of three remain with the lower parts of the walls at Oakham.

Dating from the 1260s is a much smaller but strongly walled rectangular court at Barnwell in Northamptonshire with circular towers at three corners and the fourth corner having a D-shaped tower facing in one direction and a gatehouse with two U-shaped tower facing in the other. A twin-towered gatehouse of the 1250s remains of Henry III's outer bailey at Nottingham, and there is another royal gatehouse of this type of the 1270s at Rockingham. Both these gatehouses have had their upper parts rebuilt. The much smaller and more ruinous twin-towered gatehouse between the two wards at Codnor may also be 13th century. The curtain wall at Lincoln has a single mid 13th century round corner tower. Of domestic buildings of this period there are slight remains of the hall at Peveril, a much altered hall at Rockingham, and a ruined aisled hall at the bishop's palace at Lincoln.

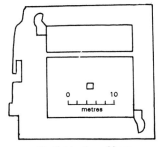

Lincoln: plan of shell keep (Lucy Tower)

Duffield: plan of keep

Several castles in the East Midlands played a major part in the civil war of King Stephen's reign (1135-54), during which the king himself was defeated and captured by a relief force whilst trying to recapture the castle at Lincoln. His successor Henry II (1154-89) attempted to exercise greater control over possession of castles. Many were dismantled soon after his accession and after his sons' rebellion of 1173-4 the castles of barons of dubious loyalty were also dismantled. The construction of embattled secular buildings was then regulated. Richard I (1189-99) began the system of licences to crenellate (embattle) being issued by kings to barons who were considered trustworthy, and unlicensed fortifications were liable to be confiscated or dismantled. Later medieval buildings can thus sometimes be dated with greater accuracy because the dates of their licences are known, and more other records have survived, although in some cases a licence was obtained without any work ensuing, or to ratify work already begun. The earliest licensed work in the East Midlands is the low outer wall of c1195 at Haddon Hall. The well-preserved mid 14th century apartments and service rooms within the wall did not require a further licence.

Henry III issued crenellation licences in 1231 and 1267 respectively for the work at Tattershall already described and for works at Belvoir which have not survived. One of the four round corner towers remains of the quadrangular moated castle at Somerton in Lincolnshire which Edward I licensed Bishop Anthony Bek to build in 1281. There is no record of a licence for the rebuilding of the early 14th century at Newark, when a new riverside wall was provided with adjoining hall blocks and two polygonal towers. Of four Northamptonshire castles licensed by Edward I, nothing medieval remains at Castle Ashby (1306), only earthworks remain at Braybrooke and Titchmarsh (both licensed in 1304), a just one altered domestic building at Thorpe Waterville (1301), although excavations have revealed the basic layout at Titchmarsh, where there were polygonal corner towers. Parts remain, with two gateways, of the cathedral precinct walls at Lincoln licensed in 1285 and 1319, and of the bishop's palace licensed in 1329, while Thornton Abbey in Lincolnshire has a huge gatehouse licensed in 1382 forming the entrance to a formerly moated precinct. Other licences issued by Edward II included Folkingham (1312) and Whitwick (1320), where only earthworks remain, and Melbourne (1311), where a length of wall remains of a quadrangular building. The single rectangular tower of an assumed quadrangular court with corner towers at Grimsthorpe in Lincolnshire is probably also of this period.

Wingfield Manor

Newark Castle

Drayton in Northamptonshire, licensed by Edward III in 1328, has retained an altered hall and solar block lying between two walled courts, one of which is fairly intact. Just a length of wall remains of a quadrangular court with round corner towers at Gresley in Nottinghamshire, licensed in 1340, and only earthworks remain of Moor End, licensed in 1347, and much improved by Edward III himself in the 1360s. Other buildings of this period were the Bishop of Lincoln's palace at Lyddington in Rutland (licensed in 1336 but entirely rebuilt later), South Kyme in Lincolnshire, which has a lofty square solar tower probably of the 1360s, Codnor in Derbyshire, which has mid 14th century walling with projecting latrine turrets in both the inner and outer wards, and Fotheringhay in Northamptonshire, where the late 14th century shell keep and curtain wall have gone, although the fine original motte and bailey remain. At Ashby-de-la-Zouch are ruins of a large status-symbol kitchen tower was added c1360 to an older unfortified manor house retaining work of several periods. Nottinghamshire has a group of small 14th century solar towers at Apsley, Halloughton, Linby, and Strelley. They were unlicensed and there is no certainty that any of them were embattled. Apsley has gone and only Halloughton remains fairly unaltered.

Lofty machicolated tower houses containing suites of private rooms for their lords were added to the older castle at Tattershall c1433-47 and to the previously unfortified manor house at Ashby-de-la-Zouch (licensed 1474). Ashby is ashlar-faced, whilst Tattershall is of brick with stone dressings, although it contains moulded brick vaults. Both have machicolations at the summit and polygonal corner turrets, those at Tattershall rising the full height of the building and containing useful chambers. The Ashby tower was capable of being defended independently but the Tattershall tower had separate entrances to rooms on different storeys and could not be defended for more than a few hours against an enemy in the main courtyard. Tattershall was the work of Lord Cromwell, who built also built the huge ruined mansion with ranges around inner and outer courts and a high tower at Wingfield in Derbyshire. Near Tattershall he built another brick tower, the Tower on the Moor, with a polygonal staircase corner turret. This seems to have been the model for a group of brick tower houses around Boston. One has been destroyed but those at Hussey and Rochford still stand high. There is also an octagonal brick tower at Gainsborough Old Hall.

The base of the great tower at Tattershall

Lord Hastings' licence of 1474 not only included Ashby, but Bagworth, where nothing remains, and Kirby Muxloe, where a 14th century manor house on a moated platform with a gatehouse was replaced in 1481-4 by a larger platform supporting a quadrangular brick structure with square corner towers and a large gatehouse with octagonal corner turrets. Both the gatehouse (left unfinished in 1484) and the single surviving corner tower feature gunports, a feature that had first appeared in English castellated buildings further south a century earlier. Other 15th century buildings are the gatehouses of the manor houses at Astwell in Northamptonshire and Mackworth in Derbyshire. Of late medieval modifications to older buildings the most notable are the two gatehouses of an new outer enclosure at Leicester, an oriel added to a remodelled hall at Newark, the new chapel of c1470 at Ashby-de-la-Zouch, plus the base of a huge semi-octagonal tower added by Richard III at Nottingham. Edward IV added a suite of lodgings at Nottingham which have vanished and also granted licences for the crenellation of the Northamptonshire houses of Boughton (1473) and Bradden (1477). Both retain old parts although it is doubtful if either have anything going back quite as early as the period of the licences. Two ranges at Haddon Hall and the gateway tower in the angle between them are of the late 15th and early 16th centuries, whilst the chapel there contains early 15th century work.

Many medieval houses were provided with moats and a fashion for them lasted well into the 16th century. Moats did not require licences and a distinction between sites that are fortified and those that are not is not always easy to make. A change of status either from house to castle or from castle to unfortified house was not unknown. Water filled ditches were not necessarily military in purpose. A moat was a permanent and efficient boundary for keeping vagrants, wild animals and malefactors out of manorial enclosures, and would also have been useful to control the comings and goings of domestic animals, servants and members of the family if the only possible access was through a gatehouse always manned by a porter or guard. At all periods were appreciated as scenic features, and served as a habitat for fish, eels and water fowl, although separate fish-ponds (fish-stews) were often provided since moats were quite often used to flush latrine systems.

In the medieval period castle walls of rubble were sometimes limewashed outside, making them look very different to the way they appear today. Dressed stones around windows and doorways would be left uncovered. Domestic rooms would have had whitewashed walls decorated with murals of biblical, historical or heroic scenes mostly painted in red, yellow and black. By the 14th century wall hangings decorated with the same themes came into fashion. Although used in churches, glass was very expensive, and although it is occasionally mentioned in building accounts it was not that common in secular buildings before the 15th century, so windows were originally closed with shutters. As a result rooms were dark when the weather was too cold or wet for the shutters to be opened for ventilation. In the later medieval period large openings in the outer walls sometimes had iron bars or grilles protecting them even if high off the ground. Living rooms usually had fireplaces although some halls head central hearths with the smoke escaping through louvres in the roof. Latrines were commonly provided in the thickness of the walls and help to indicate which rooms were intended for living or sleeping in, rather than just storage space.

Furnishings were quite sparse up until the 15th century, although the embrasures of upper storey windows often have built-in seats. Lords with several castles and houses tended to circulate around them administering their manorial courts and consuming agricultural produce on the spot. They might also be away for long periods at court or on military or diplomatic service. Their wives or junior family members might be left in residence but often castles were left almost empty for long periods, gradually crumbling away with only a skeleton staff in residence to administer the estates. Even today the monarchy still to some degree follows this nomadic pattern, having several residences, each used at certain times or for specific activities. Servants and clerks often travelled with their lords and sometimes portable furnishings kept in wooden chests such as rugs, wall-hangings and bedding, and perhaps also cooking utensils, were carried around with their owners. The lord and his immediate family had their own rooms and could have privacy when they wanted it. In the later medieval period castles had ranges of lodgings for household officials and guests with their retinues. Servants and retainers enjoyed less privacy, sharing of beds and communal sleeping in the hall or any other warm places being common.

Kitchen Tower at Ashby-de-la-Zouch   *Lincoln Bishop's Palace: the kitchen*

Records of castles needing urgent repairs abound from the 13th century onwards. After the breakdown of the original system of mandatory annual periods of garrison duty for lesser landowners, garrisons were only provided at times of unrest since they were expensive. Even the strongest fortresses were sometimes captured easily because their defences were in a ruinous state, or because it was not possible to adequately provision and man them before they were attacked, or because those within decided for whatever reason not to offer more than a token resistance. Castles with large single enclosures such as Lincoln, Northampton, and Oakham would have required two hundred men or more to fully man all the walls against a determined attack and medieval garrisons were usually much smaller than this. These royal castles were used by sheriffs whose personal armed retinue would provide basic security for the safe keeping of prisoners and stocks of munitions. Smaller enclosures with very high walls like Newark would have been much easier to defend.

Most of the castles described in this book fell into ruin before the end of the medieval period and are described as such by Henry VIII's topographer John Leland. At the royal castles in county towns such as Leicester, Lincoln and Northampton rooms were maintained for the holding of courts and keeping of prisoners after everything else was allowed to fall into ruin. On the whole the more recent tower houses and fortified houses fared better, and a fair number remain roofed today. None of the early 16th century work at Belvoir survives but parts of Grimsthorpe are of that period, although much altered. Drayton, Haddon and Rockingham have much work of the second half of the 16th century, including long galleries then in fashion. In the early 17th century Bolsover was totally remodelled into a romantic folly with a new self contained suite replacing the medieval keep and two new ranges around an outer ward, one of which again contains a long gallery, whilst some of the rooms at Ashby-de-la-Zouch were also remodelled in the early 17th century.

Haddon Hall

Fireplace at Ashby-de-la-Zouch   *Gateway arch at Kirby Muxloe*

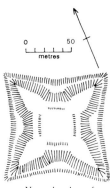

Newark: plan of
Queen's Sconce

Queen's Sconce at Newark

Ashby, Belvoir, Bolsover, Bolingbroke, Newark, Nottingham, Rockingham and Wingfield suffered sieges during the Civil War of the 1640s. All suffered some degree of dismantling by order of Parliament afterwards, ranging from the removal of doors and parapets at Bolsover, the demolition of half of the defensive circuits at Ashby and Rockingham, where in each case the domestic buildings were saved, through to the almost total destruction of Belvoir and Nottingham. At Northampton the castle and town walls survived the Commonwealth period of the 1650s only to suffer destruction by order of Charles II in 1662. Belvoir (where no medieval work remains visible) and Haddon are stately homes opened to the public by their owner, the Duke of Rutland. Castle Ashby (where no medieval work remains) and Grimsthorpe are other stately homes open to the public. The tower at Tattershall which was restored from ruin in the early 20th century is a National Trust property. Ashby-de-la-Zouch, Bolingbroke, Kirby Muxloe, Lincoln bishop's palace, Peveril and Wingfield are in the care of English Heritage, which also looks after Bolsover, where parts are roofed and other parts have been ruined since the late 18th century. Part of Wingfield still forms a farm, and this is true also of Codnor and Somerton. Maintained by local authorities are the castles at Lincoln, Newark and Oakham, the more fragmentary remains at Leicester and Nottingham, Gainsborough Old Hall, and earthworks at Bourne, Hinkley, Lilbourne, Long Buckby and Sleaford. The much-altered Northamptonshire houses of Astwell, Boughton and Bradden, plus three tower houses in Nottinghamshire remain in use as private dwellings. The ruins at Barnwell, Mackworth and South Kyme are also private although the last two can be viewed at fairly close quarters. Many earthworks can be viewed from roads, paths or public spaces and, in particular, there is access to the earthworks at Laxton and Fotheringhay, and the sites of Donnington and Mountsorrel.

Last remains of the keep at Duffield

GAZETTEER OF CASTLES IN DERBYSHIRE

BAKEWELL CASTLE   SK 221688   F

On a west-facing spur above the east side of the town is a small motte with a dished top with slight traces of two baileys.

BOLSOLVER CASTLE   SK 471707   E

It was probably the second of three successive William Peverils that founded this castle in the early 12th century. The third William was taken prisoner along with King Stephen at the battle of Lincoln in 1141 and was forfeited in 1155 by Henry II for his alleged involvement in the poisoning of the Earl of Chester. Most of the £116 spent by the king on the castles of Peveril and Bolsover probably went on building a small keep at the latter. This would have been the tower repaired by Richard I in 1194, after the rebellious Prince John had forfeited it. As king John did further work on it in 1208. Custody of the castle was granted in 1216 to William de Ferrers, Earl of Derby, but Gerard de Furnival refused to hand it over. The earl only got possession after he had besieged the castle and breached the inner curtain wall. In 1223 a new tower was added to fill the breach and another tower was erected in 1228 to replace a section of the curtain that had fallen. A new kitchen and barn were also erected during that period. In 1249-53 Henry III spent £148 on repairs to the upper parts of the keep, the roof of the queen's chamber, and to the foundations of the curtain wall.

After 1290 the castle and manor were farmed out to series of absentee landlords and the buildings quickly fell into decay. Henry VI granted Bolsover to Edmund Tudor, and it passed to his brother Jasper Tudor, Earl of Pembroke, and then reverted to the Crown. Henry VIII granted it to the Duke of Norfolk but it reverted to the Crown again when his son the Earl of Surrey was executed and attainted in 1547.

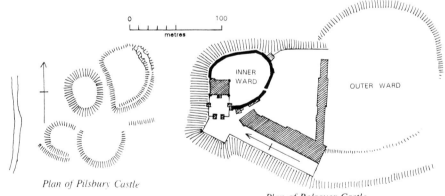

Plan of Pilsbury Castle

Plan of Bolsover Castle

The motte at Bakewell

The inner ward curtain wall at Bolsover

In 1553 Bolsover was granted to Sir George Talbot, who succeeded as 6th Earl of Shrewsbury in 1560. The 7th Earl, Gilbert, granted a long lease of the castle to his brother-in-law Charles Cavendish in 1608. Charles was a son of the celebrated Bess of Hardwick by the second of her four marriages and inherited her enthusiasm for constructing fine buildings. At Bolsover he replaced the medieval keep with a splendid new structure designed by Robert Smithson known as the Little Castle. Charles Cavendish was succeeded in 1617 by his son William, who was created Viscount Mansfield by James I. In 1633 he was made Earl of Newcastle by Charles I, whom he entertained at Bolsover in 1634. Earl William built a fine new suite of apartments on the west side of the outer court, and a building to contain a riding school on the south side. The earl was a leading Royalist commander in the Civil War, but he went into exile abroad after the defeat at Marston Moor and in August Colonel Muschamp and the garrison at Bolsover surrendered on terms and marched out with most of their equipment, although they left behind "six pieces of ordnance and three hundred firearms". In 1649 the castle was demilitarised by removing its outworks and heavy doors, but the apartments remained intact until the building was sold for the value of its materials. The earl finally returned at Charles II's restoration in 1660 and in 1665 was made Duke of Newcastle. The building needed considerable repair after its repurchase and only during the last few years before his death in 1676 was the duke able to peacefully enjoy the completed building. The title became extinct on the death of the second Duke in 1691 but it was eventually created anew for John Holles, Earl of Clare, who married his heiress, Margaret. Upon her death in 1716 the castle passed to her daughter Henrietta. She and her husband, Edward Harley, Earl of Oxford mostly lived at Welbeck Abbey and in the 1750s the west wing at Bolsover was again stripped of its roof for reuse at Welbeck, although the Little Castle remained in use as an occasional retreat. The castle then passed by marriage to the Duke of Portland. It was placed in State care by the 7th Duke of Portland in 1945.

The west side of Bolsover Castle

The rampart and ditch of the medieval town of Bolsover formed a D-shape 400m wide with a 600m long straight SW side set above a steep drop. An extension to the enclosed area was later made at the SE end, beyond where the church lies. A deep gully penetrates into the centre of the D to provide a strong promontory at the west corner upon which the castle was situated. It consisted of a stone walled bailey about 60m by 50m set on the end of the promontory and an irregularly shaped outer bailey 160m across in each direction lying between it and the town. The Riding School range of the 1630s divided off a triangular space known as the Great Court from the rest of the outer bailey in which were located the stables and barns, most of which seem to have been dismantled in the 1650s and have left no remains. The Riding School and the harness room east of it remain roofed but the smithy to the west is ruinous. The spectacular west range containing the main 17th century apartments is also ruined. The north end contained private rooms over kitchens and service rooms, and then further south was a dining room adapted out of a former hall. Beyond was a huge entrance hall created in the late 1630s and two more rooms at the south end. Backed against these rooms, placed so as to face the fine view to the west across a 15m wide terrace below, was a long gallery 54m long by 7m wide.

The 3.3m thick and 5m high enclosing wall of the Fountain Garden is the is the 12th century curtain wall of the inner court refaced (and presumably thickened) on both sides in the early 17th century so that no medieval work actually remains visible. The east and south garden rooms take the place of the towers added in the 1220s and the west garden room (actually a suite of three rooms) takes the place of the former gatehouse, which probably had twin towers flanking a central passage. The existing gateway on the south was inserted in the late 1630s.

The Little Castle of 1608-17 and its forecourt to the west replaced the medieval keep. The forecourt is 21m square and has a square tower in the middle of each long side, a twin towered gateway facing west and the Little Castle filled the east side. The Little Castle is a remarkable Jacobean castellated folly residence four storeys high with fine ceilings and other remarkable details, although a full description of its features and significance lie outside the scope of this book about medieval fortifications. There are square corner turrets, except that the NE corner has a tower containing a stair and rising above the rest of the building, and there is a projecting west porch reached by steps from the forecourt. In the basement are the servant's hall, a kitchen and other service rooms. Above are a hall and another chamber with a central pillar, whilst on the north side at third storey level is the Star Chamber.

BRETBY CASTLE   SK 293232

Extending SW of the church, towards Bretby Farm, are confused earthworks of a former stone castle of two enclosures which is mentioned in a document of 1353. It was dismantled by Philip Stanhope, Earl of Chesterfield, whose new mansion of c1610 lies in extensive grounds nearby.

CASTLE GRESLEY   SK 284178

Only a mound called Castle Knob remains of this seat of the Gresley family, owners of the manor since the late 11th century. It seems to have been no more than a site by the 1370s, and the family subsequently lived at Drakelow. Some remains of the castle seem to have survived at the time of Camden's visit in the 1580s.

Domestic building at Codnor

CODNOR CASTLE   SK 434500   V

Henry, son of a John de Grey mentioned in 1211, obtained Codnor by marrying Isolda, heiress of the Codnor family. Most of the present remains are likely to have been built in the 1330s or 40s by a John de Grey who served under Edward III in his Scottish wars. On the death of Henry, last Baron Grey of Codnor in 1496 his estates passed to Lord Zouch of Harringworth's son John, who had married Henry's aunt, Elizabeth. The Zouches sold the castle in 1634 to the Neile family and in 1692 they sold it to Sir Streynsham Masters. Most of the castle was then ruinous and Sir Streynsham lived in what is now the farmhouse on the east side of the outer court. The Masters family sold the estate to the Butterly Iron Company and much of it has since been quarried away, although the castle and its environs have survived.

The castle consisted of an inner ward about 45m long from north to south by 30m wide and an outer ward extending more than 50m to the south. There appear to have been wet moats although the surroundings have been much disturbed. On the east side of the outer ward is a farmhouse containing work of the mid 17th century and probably several other periods. A 35m long length of the west wall of the outer ward stands up to 3m high with two projecting turrets which contained pairs of latrines. This part is mid 14th century, and so is the ogee-headed window in the western part of the 1.1m thick curtain wall up to 4m high on the south side of the inner ward, where there must have been lodgings. This wall had circular corner towers about 8m in diameter, now reduced to their bases, and in the middle was a twin towered gatehouse. Only the base remains of the eastern tower but the western tower, 4m in diameter over walls 1m thick stands 4m high with two arrow-loops facing SW and SE. This part is built of large blocks rather than small slabs and could be earlier. Nothing remains of the west side of the inner ward, nor anything of the north side, where the hall must have been, but on the east side is the lower part of a 14th century wall 1.2m thick with two latrine turrets. Adjoining the northernmost of these are ruins standing up to 9m high of a rectangular block 19m long from north to south by 12m wide, but with a recess in the middle of the east side, which is destroyed to its base. This building may be 15th century, but has suffered much alteration and rebuilding. The lowest level had large fireplaces and was probably a kitchen, greatly reduced in height by the insertion of chambers above later on.

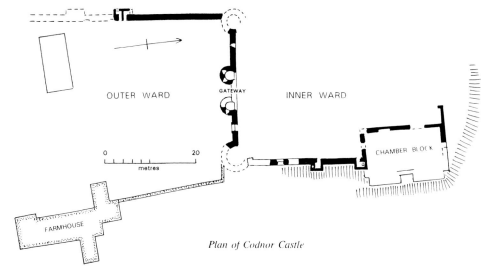

Plan of Codnor Castle

Curtain wall and gatehouse at Codnor

DERBY CASTLE   SK 355361

The names Castlefields and Castle Street support the theory that the earl of Chester had a castle at Derby in King Stephen's reign, possibly on a former mound known as Cockpit Hill SE of the town centre. Derby was fortified by the Danes and was captured by Ethelfleda in 917 but there is nothing to suggest that the medieval town had defences of any kind, and the castle was probably short-lived.

Latrine doorways at Codnor

DUFFIELD CASTLE   SK 343441   F

Set on a large but low mound measuring 75m by 50m on top, but with its western wall on solid rock, are footings revealed by excavation in 1886 of one of England's largest tower keeps, measuring almost 30m from east to west by 28m over walls 4.5m thick. The lowest steps of spiral stairs were once visible in the SE and NW corners, and there is a well near the SW corner. An east-west crosswall divided the interior so that each of the upper storeys contained a hall to the south with a chamber to the north. A central pier helped to support the hall floor. There appeared to be some sort of forebuilding against the west side. The building seems to have been destroyed by fire and is assumed to have suffered destruction by Henry II as a consequence of William de Ferrers' participation in the rebellion of 1173-4. The earthworks, which include a bailey platform on the west side, may go back to the time of Henry de Ferrers, who died in 1089, and the keep was probably built in the 1120s or 30s. Robert de Ferrers, whose earldom of Derby was forfeited in 1266 by Henry III for a rebellion which ended in his defeat at Chesterfield, may have refortified the site. Excavations in 1957 found 13th century pottery and showed that the ditch south of the mound was later recut with a wide flat bottom. See pages 7 and 13.

GLOSSOP CASTLE   SK 028955   F

Quarrying has damaged a ringwork on the end of a ridge and removed all traces of a possible bailey. A ditch around the NE end is the most obvious relic.

The hall at Haddon Hall   *The NW tower at Haddon Hall*

HADDON HALL   SK 235664   O

The Vernon family inherited Haddon by marriage c1170 and in 1195 Richard Vernon obtained a licence from Richard I to enclose his house with an uncrenellated wall 12 feet high. Remnants of it survive on the east, south and west sides of the present building, which lies on a shelf above the River Derwent. It is now embattled throughout and looks rather impressive when viewed up from the approach across the river. Apart from chimney stacks and buttresses (especially those of the kitchen) the only medieval projection from the basic quadrangular shape of 70m by 40m is the chapel at the SW corner, originally the parish church of Nether Haddon. The chapel is also partly of the 1190s with lancets of that date in the two bay south aisle. It also has a narrow north aisle, east of which is a staircase surmounted by an octagonal turret of c1450. The clerestory and the chancel with a five-light east window are of 1427. The chapel has medieval glass, wall paintings and many old furnishings.

The present main entrance is now under a four storey NW tower with a polygonal stair turret corbelled out over the SW corner. The tower was built along with the three north range by Sir Henry Vernon c1500, after he had already built the two storey west range to provide lodgings for retainers. This gateway has an awkward squinch arch over its portal towards the lower (or western) court, which is reached from it only by steps, necessitating leaving horses at the stables down below. The original main entrance was that immediately south of the Eagle Tower at the NE corner of the mansion, which leads into the upper (or eastern) court.

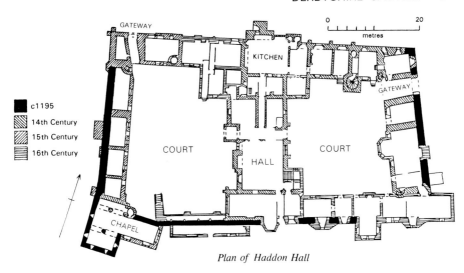

Plan of Haddon Hall

The hall range dividing the upper and lower courts was built in the mid 14th century by another Richard Vernon, and most of the range on the north side of the upper court is also his work. The hall is 9m wide internally but only 12.5m long including the screens passage at the north end. This has a fine screen of c1450 and three doorways to a pantry, buttery and a passage between them to the kitchen beyond. The kitchen has fireplaces in the west and north walls and originally extended through two storeys. A room to the east contains two ovens. Over these service rooms are chambers, one of which has access to the gallery extending not only over the screens passage but over the east side of the hall to communicate with the great chamber over the parlour at the south end. The hall west porch forms a tower containing two upper rooms. On this side the hall has two-light mid 14th century windows on either side of a fireplace, and the parlour has a west window of c1500. The east side of the hall has just one window and access to a scale- and-platt staircase to an upper lobby, off which is reached the great chamber.

Also reached from the lobby is along gallery taking up all of the south side of the upper court. Both the stair and gallery were built c1600 by Sir John Manners, husband of Dorothy Vernon, who had inherited the hall on the death of her father Sir George Vernon in 1567. The gallery looks out upon the terraced gardens created in the 17th century and projects out beyond the main east wall. It also has a rectangular bay on the south between two smaller polygonal bays, all of them with mullion-and-transom windows. At the same time a bay window was added to the west side of the east range of the upper court, the great chamber over the parlour was given large new windows, and three oriel windows were also provided for what probably once formed a smaller and older gallery to the west of the great chamber. This older gallery was perched upon the old outer wall thickened up below by adding thin rooms alongside it, and is now called the Earl's Apartments, since it was later divided up into a suite of rooms used by Sir John Manners, who succeeded to the earldom of Rutland in 1641. The family were elevated to the dukedom of Rutland in 1703 and about that time Belvoir became their chief residence. Somehow Haddon managed to survive without either falling into total ruin or being drastically remodelled during the 18th and 19th centuries, hence its great value today as a little-altered late medieval and Tudor mansion. It is still owned by the present Duke of Rutland.

HATHERSAGE CASTLE   SK 234819   V

The 60m diameter Camp Green ringwork containing two houses east of the church has ramparts on the north and east sides.

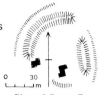

Plan of Camp Green at Hathersage

HOLMSFIELD CASTLE   SK 319776   V

A small motte lies behind the church hall west of the church.

HOPE CASTLE   SK 171834   V

A stream has eroded the interior of a ringwork 50m across west of the church.

HORSTON CASTLE   SK 376432

The de Buron family had a castle here which passed in 1198 to Peter de Sandiacre, but in 1199 he surrendered it to King John in exchange for other lands in Derbyshire. The king spent over £700 on improvements and in 1205 there is a mention of "crenellating our tower of Harestan". As early as 1713 the site had been much disturbed by quarrying and remains of the castle are minimal, but there is part of the sloping base (with a mural chamber) of an ashlar-faced keep (no doubt the tower mentioned above), built on a boss of rock. It seems to have been pentagonal, or a square with a prow on one side, like the keep at Mitford in Northumberland. In 1214 King John allowed the wife of William de Ferrers, Earl of Derby to reside in the castle whilst the earl was on crusade in the Holy Land. Henry III's Pipe Rolls refer to a gate, barbican, bridges, and a hall and chapel. In the 1250s the castle was held in turn by Peter de Montfort and then Hugh Despencer, and in 1254 it was captured by Robert de Ferrers for Simon de Montfort. In 1392 Horston (also called Horsley) was granted by Richard II to John de Holland, Earl of Huntingdon. It was later granted to the Earl of Richmond, and after Henry VII came to the throne the castle, probably by then ruinous, went to Jasper Tudor, Earl of Pembroke. In 1514 Henry VIII granted Horston to the Duke of Norfolk, and he in 1530 conveyed it to Sir Michael Stanhope, whose descendants, later earls of Chesterfield, held the manor until c1817.

The last remains of the keep at Horston   **The gatehouse at Mackworth**

The last remaining wall of Melbourne Castle

MACKWORTH CASTLE SK 311378 V

All that remains of the seat of the Mackworth family is the frontage of a modest late 15th century gatehouse. Sir Thomas Mackworth, whose chief seat was at Normanton in Rutland, was created a baronet by James I in 1619, and in 1655 his grandson Sir Thomas sold the manor to Sir John Curzon. The gatehouse is embattled with tiny round bartizans on the two surviving outer corners, and has buttresses at the corners and on either side of the portal, which has an ogival hoodmould. The passage was flanked by rooms for guards or porters. Above was a suite of rooms with square-headed windows of two lights facing the field.

MELBOURNE CASTLE SK 389252

A 20m length of 4m high walling, ivy covered on one side and obscured by outbuildings on the other, remains in a garden. The castle was built by Robert de Holland, who in 1311 obtained a licence to crenellate it from Edward II. When the latter had de Holland attainted in 1321 the castle passed to Thomas, Earl of Lancaster, who had owned the manor prior to its transfer to de Holland. He was executed the same year but his brother Henry managed to inherit the estate. On the death of his son Henry in 1361 Melbourne passed to his daughter Blanche, whose husband John of Gaunt, a younger son of Edward III, was created Duke of Lancaster. On Henry IV's accession in 1399 the duchy was merged with the crown. John, Duke of Bourbon, captured during Henry V's victory at Agincourt was kept prisoner in the castle for 18 years until a ransom of £30,000 was paid, but the duke died before he got back to France. Leland c1540 describes the castle as "in metely repair", but forty years later Camden found that the custodian, the Earl of Huntingdon, had allowed it to decay. The earl obtained an outright grant of the manor from James I in 1604. A sketch of the castle made during this period shows it having a square gatehouse, a dozen round and square turrets, and an array of elaborate chimney stacks.

MORLEY CASTLE SK 397408 and 397408

There is a small motte near the church and another with a wet moat on Morley Moor.

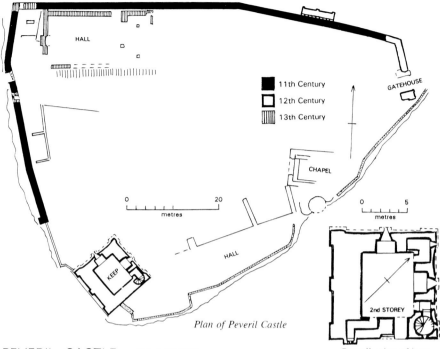

Plan of Peveril Castle

Peveril: plan of keep

PEVERIL CASTLE   SK 149826

This castle takes its present name from William Peveril, who is recorded in the Domesday Book of 1086 as holding a castle here. Closing off the north side of a triangular headland about 80m by 60m with sheer drops on the other two sides is a wall 1.5m thick with a damaged wall-walk 5m above the steeply sloping ground outside. The lower part of the parapet also survives. Since there are no signs of any earthwork defences for the main courtyard this wall may well go back to c1075-85, especially since it includes sections of herringbone masonry, usually dated to the 11th century or not much later. The slightly thicker curtain wall on the west side now standing about 2.5m high is thought to be the work of his son William, who succeeded c1114 and lost his estates forty years later when Henry II accused him of poisoning the Earl of Chester. There is high ground beyond the chasm on this side, from which missiles could be fired into the court but for the presence of this screen wall. This high ground has slight traces of an outer court enclosed by a bank and ditch. The original main gate where the keep now stands faced towards this court.

Henry II visited the castle in 1157 and 1158, and again in 1164, when King Malcolm IV came and offered his submission. Henry's Pipe Rolls record £135 being spent on the tower in the castle of Pech (Peak) in 1176. It seems that in 1174 work had begun on replacing the original gatehouse with the present keep, and that a new entrance (now destroyed) was made alongside it, whilst a second entrance, the jambs of which remain, was built at the NE corner, together with a slim projection 7m wide with three pilaster buttresses added to flank the eastern section of the north curtain wall. The lost arch of the NE gateway is known to have been decorated with chevrons. About the same time the village of Castleton far below to the north was provided with a rampart and ditch, still surviving on the north and west sides.

The keep measures 11.7m square above a plinth which only survives on the west, since it was built against a rock platform on the south and the whole of the lower parts of the north and east sides have been robbed of their fine ashlar facing. There are pilaster buttresses at the corners and in the middle of each face, except the south. The interior rooms are rectangular since the vulnerable west wall is more massive than the other three walls, which are 2.6m thick at basement level. The entrance doorway, with evidence of a drawbar slot, lies in the south wall and admits to the upper room, which has windows facing north and east, a third window at a higher level on the south, and a latrine corbelled out at the SW corner. A spiral stair leads down to the basement, which has loops facing north and east, and up to the wall-walk some 15m above the sloping ground to the north but only 10.5m above the rock platform to the south. On three sides the lower part of the parapet still survives. The only opening in the west wall is a dummy window above roof level.

Peveril was amongst the many castles which Richard I handed over to his brother Prince John. During his reign from 1199 John spent minor sums on repairing it. After his death the castle seems to have fallen into the hands of rebels and was besieged and captured in 1217 by William de Ferrers, Earl of Derby on half of the young Henry III. The king visited the castle in 1235 and in 1251 ordered the recovering with lead of the roof of the keep, and repairs to a new tower, the bakehouse and the porch of the old hall. The new tower must have been either the circular tower about 6m in diameter, half of the base of which remains on the southern cliff edge, or the larger larger D-shaped tower of which slight traces remain on the cliff further east, near the keep. The towers formed part of a new curtain then added on this side which has vanished and been replaced by a thin modern parapet. Why towers were provided on this side instead of on the more vulnerable northern side is a mystery. There are footings of what is thought to have been an early chapel to the north of the eastern tower and between it and the keep is a longer footing of the 11th and 12th century hall block. This was the old hall mentioned in 1251, by which time a new hall measuring 16m by 10.4m had been built on the made-up ground behind the western part of the north curtain. Space was left for a chamber in the NW corner, where there is a late 13th century opening in the curtain wall. Only footings remain of the hall, with a fireplace at the west end and an open hearth in the middle, and still less of the service rooms east of it. Other rooms of this period extended along the west curtain.

Peveril Castle from the south

Pilsbury Castle Hills

In 1254 Henry granted the castle to his son Prince Edward and it was then given in dower to his wife Eleanor of Castile. There is a record of twelve oaks being taken in 1288 from the surrounding forest "for the repair of the houses of the King's castle of the Peak". During Edward II's reign the castle was alternately held by John de Warenne, Earl of Surrey and Queen Isabella. Edward III in turn granted the castle to his consort Philippa of Hainault in 1331 and he visited the castle that year. He later granted it to his son John of Gaunt in exchange for other estates and the castle thus became part of the Duchy of Lancaster merged with the Crown since 1399. Excavations have failed to reveal any later pottery and it seems the castle was abandoned about then. It has been in State guardianship as a monument since 1932.

PILSBURY CASTLE   SK 114638   V

This is a rather curious site with a motte about 4m high and 28m across on top lying east of the River Dove. A D-shaped bailey extends 45m to where there are three rocky crags. These rise higher than the motte but only partly shielded it from the higher ground not far to the east. There are two other enclosures on the south side.

WINGFIELD MANOR   SK 374547   E

Excavations have revealed traces of a 12th century stone curtain wall upon this promontory site, a relic of a castle belonging to William Peveril forfeited to Henry II in 1155. Wingfield was then given to William de Heriz, only to be temporarily confiscated when he failed to support the king's expedition to Ireland in 1171. The manor eventually passed to Roger Bellars and after his death there was a legal battle over its possession between Henry VI's Chancellor, Ralph, Lord Cromwell, and Sir Henry Pierrepont, who were both descendants of John, the last of the Heriz male line. It was finally settled with Lord Cromwell getting Wingfield and Sir Henry various other estates. By 1439 Lord Cromwell had built the hall, kitchen and lodgings forming the heart of the present mansion, and work continued, with several changes of plan, on the rest of the building up until 1455, when just before his death he sold the still incomplete building, which he had probably never stayed in, to John Talbot, 2nd Earl of Shrewsbury. He inhabited the building and continued to work on it, but was killed fighting on the Lancastrian side at the battle of Northampton in 1460.

The inner gateway at Wingfield Manor

Just three weeks before he died at Wingfield in 1541, George, 4th Earl of Shrewsbury had invited Henry VIII to stay at the manor and enjoy the hunting around Duffield. George, 6th Earl of Shrewsbury was the fourth husband of the celebrated Bess of Hardwick, and had custody of the captive Mary, Queen of Scots. During her long imprisonment amongst his various castles and houses Mary spent several periods at Wingfield. After the death in 1616 of the 7th Earl, Gilbert, Wingfield became the residence of the Earl and Countess of Pembroke, although the Countess's two sisters also each owned a third share in it. The earl supported the Parliamentary cause but the manor was occupied by a party of Royalists sent by the Earl of Newcastle. In 1644 they were besieged by a Parliamentary force and, although the manor only really ranked as a stronghouse rather than a castle, its naturally strong position was such that it was only captured after the attackers were reinforced with heavy artillery. The building was then rendered untenable. In 1678 the manor was sold to the Halton family but they only seem to have used the hall and the rooms immediately adjacent to it. In the late 18th century Immanuel Halton moved out to a new house near the village and Wingfield was leased to farmers.

Lord Cromwell was extremely rich and Wingfield Manor is one of the largest of English medieval houses, extending for 120m from north to south and with a greatest width of 75m at the south end of the outer court. The great hall lies near the end of the promontory so it was necessary to cross both the outer and inner courts to reach it. The planning of the building is somewhat irregular and although the inner gatehouse lies in the middle of the range dividing the courts the outer gatehouse is not placed opposite it but is set at the south end of the east side of the outer court. Both gateways have separate archways for carts and pedestrians. The inner gateway has square turrets on the outer side. They are solid below but have loops above, those in the western turret being cross-shaped. The turrets form part of a series of projections in the cross-range, but the others are chimney breasts with high stacks. Over the gateway outer portal are a series of heraldic panels. The part of this range east of the inner gatehouse is still used as a farmhouse and the outer court is not open to visitors. Only the outer wall remains of the lodgings along its western side, whilst it is the inner, or western wall that survives of the 10m wide east range, although footings remain of the outer wall. The outer gatehouse has turrets 3m square containing tiny rooms, and the twin passageways are flanked by narrow rooms with fireplaces for guards or porters. Of the south range only a large barn at the east end was completed and later farmbuildings cover the site of the SW corner. The barn has a residential upper floor and a three storey tier of rooms at the east end with fireplaces. This is the only part to retain original 15th century roof timbers.

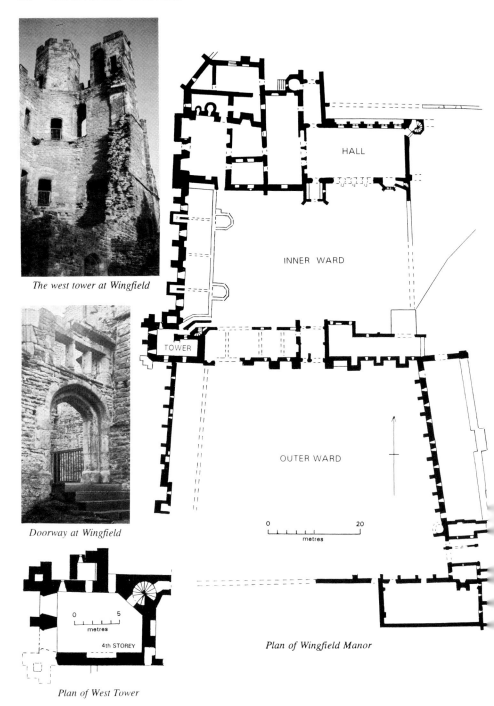

The west tower at Wingfield

Doorway at Wingfield

Plan of West Tower

4th STOREY

HALL

INNER WARD

TOWER

OUTER WARD

Plan of Wingfield Manor

The inner court measured 41m by 29m not inclusive of the ranges on all four sides. The north end of the east range was intended to contain Lord Cromwell's private suite of three storeys of rooms but nothing remains of them now apart from openings from the hall and its NE staircase. The west range contained twelve lodgings for guests arranged as four rooms on each of three storeys, the east walls of which were timber-framed. Against the impressive outer wall here are a series of bold projections, the smaller ones having fireplaces backed against them and the larger ones containing tiers of latrines set side by side. The two bay windows facing the court were later additions. Squeezed into the SW corner as an afterthought is a tower 12.8m long from east to west by 9m wide and rising through five storeys to a height of 20m above the court. Most of the 2m thick west wall was destroyed at the slighting. The NW corner was heavily buttressed with a turret squeezed in between the buttresses, and the SW corner probably matched it. A wide spiral stair in the NE corner serves all the levels. Latrines for the upper rooms were provided in a turret in the re-entrant angle between the tower and west outer wall, but half of the tower second storey was itself a communal latrine reached directly from the inner court and flushed from a cistern on the roof by means of a flue in the outer wall.

The hall (21.5m by 11m) has a stair turret at the NE corner leading up and also down to a fine vaulted undercroft with a row of central piers below the hall. The north side has five late 17th century windows, the lower of two tiers inserted when the hall was subdivided into two storeys of smaller rooms. The original windows here were set above the roof of a former pentice outside. The south side is destroyed between the oriel lighting the east end dais and one of the two porches opening onto the screens passage at the west end. Heating must have been by a central hearth.

The screens passage has the usual triple doorway arrangement with a passage flanked by a pantry and buttery, below which were other service rooms. The buttery has a stair down to the hall undercroft. North of the buttery was a chamber entered off the north porch. The passage led through to a small court with two storeys of single chambers on the south side and an 8m wide by 12m long kitchen on the west. A 17th century doorway set between the large breasts of two west fireplaces now forms the visitors' entrance to the ruins. The uppermost of the south chambers had a passage over the kitchen south side to a latrine in the outer west wall. In a slightly later rebuilding most of the open court was enclosed as a passage with a second kitchen north of it, whilst the original kitchen was given new south and north walls, the latter with ovens bulging out of it. These project into the lowest of a series of three poorly lighted chambers probably for the use of kitchen staff and served presumably by internal wooden stairs. The tier of four storeys of chambers with triangular rooms west of them to the north of the small court and kitchen also may have been an afterthought. Over the pantry and buttery was a large audience chamber extending through two levels, so that there was space for a private chamber over the ante-room divided off at the north end. These upper rooms were reached by means of a spiral stair in a turret adjoining the north porch.

OTHER CASTELLATED BUILDINGS AND SITES IN DERBYSHIRE

Barton Blount Hall (SK 208347), seat of Walter Blount, created Lord Mountjoy in 1465, has a part of a moat and a much-altered brick gatehouse with polygonal turrets. Prior Overton's fine brick tower of c1440-50 at Repton (SK 304272) has angle turrets set over buttresses. There are traces of a moat at Ashford (SK 195698), and of enclosures at Torside Castle on Harrop Moss, Glossop (SK 077966) and Castle Ring on Harthill Moor (SK 221629). Tissington has a possible ringwork (SK 176523) and there are possible mottes at Brampton (SK 289716), Pinxton (SK 459568), Repton (SK 299278), Tapton (SK 392721) & Castle Farm, Youlgreave (SK 197634).

GAZETTEER OF LEICESTERSHIRE CASTLES

ASHBY-DE-LA-ZOUCH CASTLE   SK 361166   E

The manor of Ashby had a simple unfortified manor house, originally of timber, which was rebuilt in stone either in the 1150s by Philip de Beaumont, or in the 1160s by his successor Alan la Zouch, a Breton nobleman. The walls of the original solar block and parts of the hall remain from this period. The Zouche family were of some importance in the 13th century, having manors in Shropshire and Devon as well as Leicestershire, and holding such major offices as Constable of the Tower of London, Justice of Chester, and Justice of Ireland. When the Zouch senior male line failed in 1314 Ashby passed to a member of a junior branch of the Mortimer family, Sir William, of Richard's Castle in Herefordshire. He assumed the Zouch surname and was created Baron Zouch of Ashby in 1323. An inquisition after the death of Sir William's son Alan in 1347 suggests that the new solar block to the east was then under construction, and the hall, described as ruinous, was about to be rebuilt. Shortly after this the Kitchen Tower was added to the west of the original solar block, which was then relegated to service rooms, with a chamber above.

After Hugh la Zouch died in 1399 Ashby passed through the hands of several different families, the only work of this period being a northward extension of the new solar block. The manor reverted to Edward IV in 1461 after the execution of James Butler, Earl of Ormond, following his capture at the battle of Towton. In 1464 Edward IV gave Ashby to his chamberlain, William Lord Hastings, whose original seat was a moated manor house at Kirby Muxloe (see page 37). Lord Hastings then added a chapel beyond the SE corner of the solar block and walled in a court south of it. In April 1474 Edward IV granted Lord Hastings a licence for the fortification of his Leicestershire manor houses of Ashby, Kirby Muxloe and Bagworth. At Ashby an impressive new tower house was then added on the south side. Lord Hastings was executed in the Tower of London by the Duke of Gloucester shortly before the latter took the throne as Richard III in 1483. The family retained the estates and supported the Earl of Richmond, who as Henry VII visited Ashby in 1503. Lord Hastings' grandson was created Earl of Huntingdon by Henry VIII in 1529. The third earl was President of the Council of the North under Elizabeth I and the captive Mary, Queen of Scots briefly stayed at Ashby in 1569 and 1586.

Under James I, who visited Ashby in 1614 and 1617 the Earl of Huntingdon lived here in great state with a household as big as 68 people in 1609. The cost of the lavish entertainments for the second royal visit, for which another apartment block is thought to have been hastily erected, strained the family resources to the limit. Despite this there was another expensive royal visit by Charles and Queen Henrietta Maria in 1634. The 6th Earl of Huntingdon, who succeeded in 1643, took no part in the Civil War, but his younger brother Henry Hastings used the castle as a base for Royalist operations throughout the East Midlands. He improved the defences and is said to have provided an underground passage out to the Mount House built in 1644 to accommodate Irish troops and to act as an outwork. The castle was besieged by Parliamentary forces after the battle of Naseby but was regarded as too strong to storm. Starvation and plague eventually induced the garrison to surrender in February 1646. The castle was ordered to be made untenable although this was not carried out until 1649, when the outermost walls of the Hastings and Kitchen towers were undermined and blown up. The Hastings family subsequently lived at Donnington Park, although a new house called Ashby Place was built near the castle in the 1720s, and the Buck brothers' engraving of the castle in 1730 shows that the hall, solar, chapel and other domestic buildings were then still roofed. Walter Scott's novel "Ivanhoe" published in 1819, revived public interest in the ruins, which were taken into State guardianship in 1932. They are now administered by English Heritage.

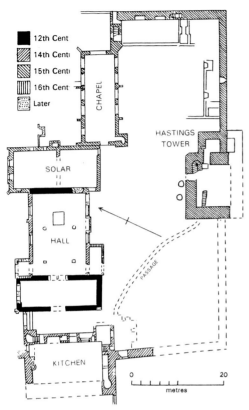

Legend:
- 12th Cent
- 14th Cent
- 15th Cent
- 16th Cent
- Later

CHAPEL

HASTINGS TOWER

SOLAR

HALL

PASSAGE

KITCHEN

0 ——————— 20
metres

Plan of Ashby-de-la-Zouch Castle

The Hastings Tower at Ashby

The castle consists of a row of domestic buildings extending from the Kitchen Tower at the west end to the chapel at the east end. The court 68m long by up to 25m wide to the south of these buildings has a 15th century curtain wall up to 1.8m thick and 4m high to the wall-walk around its east side and then along the south side as far as the Hastings Tower in the middle. The remaining sections of curtain from there round to the Kitchen Tower were probably destroyed at the slighting of 1647, except for a short stub of wall adjoining the Kitchen Tower. On the north side of the Kitchen Tower is another short stub of walling, but there is no clear evidence that it was ever continued round the whole of the northern part of the side. Although the Hastings Tower was clearly of great military strength the rest of the buildings seem to have been very inadequately defended. The 16th century gardens to the south included ornamental fishponds but there was no moat as such, and the brick corner towers of the garden, a two storey octagon at the SE, and a three storey quatrefoil at the SW, were purely ornamental, not military features. One can only assume that considerable outworks were created in the 1640s for it to be regarded as such a place of strength. At Lincoln the Parliamentary forces successfully scaled a curtain wall twice as high as that at Ashby, where the site offers no natural protection.

The Kitchen Tower at Ashby-de-la-Zouch   *The chapel at Ashby-de-la-Zouch*

The Kitchen Tower is 19m long by 13.5m wide and is mid 14th century, although the windows appear to date from a late 15th century remodelling. This is a huge building, almost the same size externally as the block further east containing an aisled hall, and had massive walls, the now-destroyed west wall being 3m thick, although a considerable wall-thickness was needed to accommodate the fireplaces with their ovens and flues. Unlike the later Hastings Tower the Kitchen Tower was not separately defensible and seems to have been a status symbol. The kitchen itself was 9m high and covered by a ribbed vault, making a very impressive chamber, with large two-light windows high up. Fireplaces with adjoining ovens remain in the east and south walls. The east wall also contains a serving hatch and a doorway with access to a spiral stair leading to a suite of well lighted rooms above the kitchen. Another doorway leads down into a cellar to the south of the tower, and an underground passageway then leads from there to the basement of the Hastings Tower.

The space east of the kitchen may have formed a court in the 14th century but was later filled in with rooms. The next building to the east is the original solar block of the 12th century hall, in the basement of which a pantry and buttery were created in the 14th century, whilst in the 16th century this part was remodelled into a structure of three storeys with mullioned windows at either end of the upper levels. As remodelled in the 14th century the hall was provided with a screens passage at the west end and arcades of two bays plus a central hearth towards the east end, where the lord's dais lay. The great width of the building suggests that the Norman hall may have had timber arcades like that at Leicester. The south porch is 16th century, whilst the west porch was added in the early 17th century, when the hall and the blocks at either end were given wide and tall new round-headed windows.

Beyond the hall is the new solar block added in the 14th century and originally containing one large upper room over two below. In the 15th century the block was lengthened at each end and provided with a fine new upper fireplace. Only a fireplace projection remains of another suite of rooms later added to the NE. The chapel is a fine structure, having four bays with three-light windows (now lacking their tracery) on either side and a five-light east window. A fifth bay at the west end contained two levels of rooms, perhaps for the priest, over a vestibule. The rooms of which foundations (and fireplaces and latrines in the curtain wall) still remain SE of the chapel are known as the Priest's Rooms, although they seem rather spacious to have served that purpose. Originally there were rooms against the south curtain and another range from there to the chapel to close off a small court at this end.

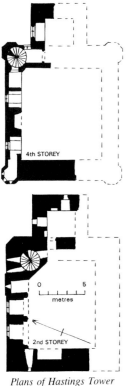

Plans of Hastings Tower

The Kitchen Tower at Ashby

The Hastings Tower has a main block 14.2m by 12.4m over walls up to 2.5m thick which contained a vaulted storage basement, a rib-vaulted kitchen, an audience chamber, and a private room at the top. A wing on the east side contained six storeys of private rooms over a strongroom, and this part seems to have contained several latrines. The tower was entered at ground level by a doorway closed by a portcullis and having two wells close by, whilst there is a third well actually within the tower. The doorway is contained in a slight projection which rises up to a canopied niche containing the Hastings arms at third storey level. From that stage upwards the surviving two corners of the main block and the remaining corner of the wing have octagonal turrets with the unusual elaboration of trefoiled blank panelling. At third storey level the NW turret contains an oriel. Only the corbelling remains of the machicolated parapets between the turrets which would have brought the original height of the building to about 25m. The upper windows were mostly of pairs of trefoiled lights under square heads with hoodmoulds. For some reason the lower part of the NE corner, which contains a spiral stair linking all the rooms, is chamfered.

BAGWORTH CASTLE

Leland in c1540 describes "ruins of a manor place, like a castle", Lord Hastings (see Ashby-de-la-Zouch having obtained a licence to fortify this site from Edward IV in 1474. There is evidence that this vanished building (its precise location is unknown) was regarded as a castle in the mid 14th century.

Ashby-de-la-Zouch   Castle

BELVOIR CASTLE   SK 820337   O

Robert de Todeni is thought to have had a castle upon this site in the 1080s. His successors, who used the surname Albini, are thought to have built a shell keep on the motte (Leland in c1540 describes a great circular keep at Belvoir) and probably a stone curtain wall. The castle was captured by King John from William de Albini in 1216 and passed by marriage to Robert de Roos in 1247. He was licensed by Henry III in 1267 to refortify the site. The castle was wrecked by Lord Hastings in 1464 after its then owner, Thomas, Lord Roos, a Lancastrian, had been executed by Edward IV, and Hastings was only able to take possession by force after a show of resistance from those within. Belvoir was restored to the Roos family by Henry VII in 1485 and passed to Sir Robert Manners, who married Eleanor, the sister of Edmund, Lord Roos, who died in 1508. Sir Robert's grandson was created Earl of Rutland by Henry VIII and in the 1520s began a rebuilding of the then still ruined castle when was completed in 1555 by the 2nd Earl.

The 5th Earl was imprisoned in the Tower of London for his part in the Earl of Essex's rebellion against Elizabeth I. He was released on her death in 1603 and entertained King James of Scotland at Belvoir when the latter came south to claim the English throne. Although the 8th Earl of Rutland sympathised with Parliament during the Civil War, Belvoir was seized by the Royalists and in 1645 was only surrendered by Sir Jervase Lucas after a four month siege. The castle was demolished in 1649, but construction of a new mansion on the site began in 1654 and continued until 1668. Queen Anne raised the earldom of Rutland to a dukedom in 1703, the 9th earl also obtaining the additional title of Marquis of Granby. The 3rd Duke added a wing in c1750 and after the 5th Duke came of age in 1801 another rebuilding was undertaken. New SW and SE facades were completed by 1816, when a fire destroyed the NE and NW sides of the mansion. These successive rebuildings have removed all medieval work, except that the Staunton Tower on the SE may contain refaced medieval work in its lower parts. Landscaping of the grounds has also destroyed all the medieval earthworks on this hilltop site, but a layout of a motte with a bailey about 100m across is to be assumed.

CASTLE DONINGTON   SK 448276   V

The site of this castle is an elevated platform about 70m across with a deep and wide ditch and counterscarp bank. A track leads across it from the south to a row of houses built on the north side of the site, and another house lies on the SE side. The castle was captured by King John in 1216, and it is mentioned in 1266, when it belonged to Henry de Lacy, Earl of Lincoln, then a minor. After the death of the last de Lacy earl of Lincoln in 1311 the castle passed to Thomas, Earl of Lancaster. After his death and execution in 1322 Donington was given by Edward II to his favourite Hugh le Despenser the younger. He in turn lost his estates when Edward II was deposed in 1326 and Donington eventually went to Edward's brother, Edmund, Earl of Kent. He was executed in 1330 but his son managed to inherit his estates. In the early 15th century Henry IV and his son Henry V both held Donington and spent small sums upon the maintenance of the castle, but it subsequently decayed. It had a stone curtain wall (a small low portion of which still remains by the row of houses) with several round and square towers. An old engraving shows a hall block with pilaster buttresses and a round-headed opening at one end.

EARL SHILTON CASTLE   SP 470982   F

A low and worn motte and traces of a large bailey lie in a park west of the church. A folly gateway on the south side of the motte has a drawbridge across the ditch.

GILMORTON MOTTE   SP 570879   F

West of the church is a low mound about 25m across on top, the ditch is which was originally water filled. There are slight traces of a kidney-shaped bailey 50m by 30m to the NW. Beyond is a moated platform of later date, so small and low that it is hardly likely to have been anything other than a garden feature or fishpond.

GROBY CASTLE   SK 524076   V

An embanked section of the A50 dual carriageway now crosses the site of a castle built in the 1140s by Robert, Earl of Leicester, and destroyed by Henry II after William de Ferrers' took part in the 1173-4 rebellion. Excavations before the destruction of the 5m high motte NE of the church showed that the site bore a manor house before it was fortified. There was a double ditch system to the north, beyond which were part of another enclosure and a fishpond, perhaps of later date, when the manor was held by the de Greys, who became Barons Ferrers of Groby. Parts of late medieval stone outbuildings are incorporated into Thomas Grey's brick Elizabethan mansion.

The motte at Gilmorton

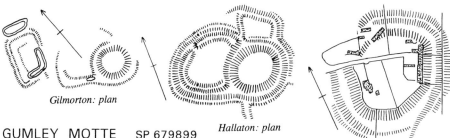

Gilmorton: plan

Hallaton: plan

0   50
metres

Castle Donington: plan

GUMLEY MOTTE   SP 679899

The Danes Camp is actually a damaged motte on a ridge between marshes.

HALLATON CASTLE   SP 780899

Castle Hill Camp is a motte and bailey lying on the end of a ridge. The motte rises 7m from a ditch to a summit 40m across. The ditch and counterscarp bank continue around a D-shaped bailey 60m by 45m with a rampart to the NW, and there is a small second enclosure to the NE.

Hinckley: plan

HINCKLEY CASTLE   SP 428938   F

In a public park is a ringwork about 60m across. The defences on the SE side are quite impressive, with a rampart rising 11m above an ornamental pond formed in the ditch. The castle is said to have been built in the 1090s by Hugh de Grentmesnil, Sheriff of Leicester. It is thought to have been held by the Earl of Leicester against Henry II in 1173 and to have been demolished after it was surrendered. The site was later reoccupied but all buildings here had vanished by the 17th century.

HUNGARTON CASTLE   SK 681049

The Monk's Grave is a small motte with a partly wet ditch.

KIBWORTH HARCOURT MOTTE   SP 681945

This motte may have been adapted from a barrow. Its bailey has been destroyed.

Gunloops at Kirby Muxloe

Fireplace in gatehouse at Kirby Muxloe

KIRBY MUXLOE CASTLE SK 524046 E

The Hastings family obtained Kirby Muxloe with the marriage of Sir Ralph to Margaret, daughter of Sir William Herle. Their son Sir Ralph built a manor house here, probably when he came of age c1355. It had a modest gatehouse and a wet moat. It was swept away for the construction of the existing castle but foundations of it still remain, indicating a hall 8.5m by 11.5m with a service passage at the south end with porches at either end and a buttery and pantry flanking a passage to a detached kitchen, and also another block from which projected a wing with a latrine turret on one side. Ralph's great gandson William was a strong supporter of Richard, Duke of York during the political struggles of the 1450s, and when York's son took the throne in 1461 as Edward IV, Sir William Hastings was appointed to the lucrative offices of Chamberlain, Master of the Mint, and Chamberlain of North Wales. That year he was summoned to Parliament as Lord Hastings, and various other honours were bestowed on him later in the reign. In 1474 he obtained from Edward IV a licence to crenellate three of his houses, including Kirby, although work there did not begin until early in 1481. The accounts record the demolition of the old buildings, the laying of foundations and completion of the new moat during the summer of 1481. Early in 1482 the existing gatehouse was begun and the "murther holles" made in April probably refer to the gunports. The new corner towers were given floors and windows during the summer and by autumn they were being roofed with lead. The work continued during the winter (which must have been unusually mild) and in January centring was erected for the vault of the gateway passage, which was built in February. In March there is a reference to foundations for a kitchen and to the making of bricks locally at the rate of 100,000 a week by Anthony "Docheman".

In April 1483 Edward IV died and in June Lord Hastings was executed in the Tower of London by the Duke of Gloucester shortly before he took the throne as Richard III. Work at Kirby almost came to a standstill during the summer but was gradually resumed at a much slower rate in the autumn. The accounts end with the temporary thatching of the gatehouse in September 1484 pending completion with a lead roof. Whether any of the building apart from the surviving corner tower was ever made habitable is uncertain. The family lived at Ashby, and Kirby passed c1630 to Sir Robert Banaster. The ruins have been a monument in State care since 1911.

The gatehouse at Kirby Muxloe from the east

Kirby Muxloe Castle

As remodelled in the 1480s Kirby Muxloe had a moat with between 15m and 23m width of water surrounding a platform 53m by 70m, from which projected corner towers 8m square. The whole building was of brick, stone only being used for foundations and the surrounds of doorways and windows. The west corner tower stands almost complete with three storeys and battlements, and the ruined gatehouse in the middle of the NW side stands two storeys high but only foundations remain of the rest of the building. The accounts suggest that considerably more than what now stands was built, even if little of it was ever properly completed. The curtain walls were set 2.5m back from the edges of the platform, allowing space for a berm with a low outer parapet between them and the moat. The berm has 10m wide midway projections and it is likely that the curtain followed the same pattern, especially since the projection on the SE side is off-centre to allow for the length of the main hall NE of it. The corner towers each had two square turrets straddling the space between the inner face of the curtain and the outer face of the berm parapet. On the surviving tower one of these turrets contains a spiral stair to the two upper storeys. The other turret contains latrines serving all three levels of lodgings each of which has a fireplace and a two-light window in the outer walls and single light windows looking along the curtain walls. The latrines had their own pits and were not flushed by the moat. The lowest level also has two keyhole-shaped gunports in each outer face and one in each of the faces flanking the berm parapet. Either from the beginning or as a modification shortly afterwards the ports were blocked to prevent draughts, but possibly with the intention that they could be opened out again in wartime.

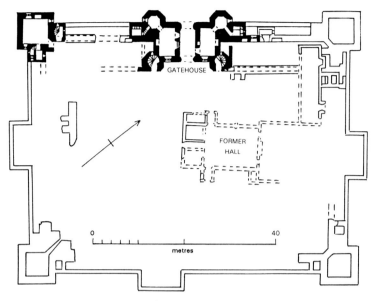

Plan of Kirby Muxloe Castle

The gatehouse is built of red bricks with patterns plus the initials W and H over the gateway, and the Hastings arms on the southern turret, executed in black bricks. The building stands ruinously to 12m above the moat although much of the inner wall of the single large room on the upper storey is missing. It measures 14.5m by 8.5m and has octagonal towers 5m in diameter facing the field and similar turrets 4.2m in diameter containing spiral staircases on the corners within the court. The outer turrets have circular gunports with sighting slits above and have adjoining them square latrine turrets where the curtain wall and berm parapet joined them. The passage has a portcullis groove and was designed for two pairs of doors, the outermost of which survive in a very decayed state with a wicket gate in one leaf. The vault of the passage has fallen, although the flanking rooms for the porters and guards retain theirs. These rooms also each have one gunport. The upper room had a pair of two-light windows facing the moat and a row of four such windows facing the court, and there are fireplaces at each end. Nothing remains of a third storey but it is likely that it existed, even if it was never roofed, for the accounts describe stones from Swarkestone Bridge being recut probably for machicolations on top of the gatehouse just before Lord Hastings was executed in April 1483. The ranges on either side of the gatehouse were clearly designed to have two storeys. That on the north had a projection from the curtain wall which blocked the berm passage.

KIRKBY MALLORY CASTLE   SK 454018

Little now remains of a once impressive earthwork here.

LAUNDE MOTTE   SK 583047

This is a small, unimpressive mound.

LEICESTER CASTLE   SK 583041   V

William I built a castle over the south corner of the Roman walled town of Leicester probably in 1068, and put it into the custody of Hugh de Grentemesnel. His son Ivo was fined so heavy for rebelling against Henry I in 1101 that his estates had to be mortgaged to Robert de Beaumont, who eventually took possession. It is thought that Henry I later made de Beaumont Earl of Leicester, and the latter may have begun to refortify the castle in stone. The church of St Mary de Castro, originally the castle chapel lying in the middle of the bailey, retains parts of a large cruciform building of c1120. The fine aisled hall built c1150 on the west side of the bailey, above the River Soar, survived the destruction of defences of the castle and town in 1174 after they were besieged and captured by Henry II, the earl having joined the princes' rebellion.

The castle later passed to Simon de Montfort, who married Henry III's sister Eleanor and was created Earl of Leicester in 1239. He ruled the kingdom for a year after his victory over the king in 1264, but was defeated and killed at the battle of Evesham in 1265. His sons were dispossessed for carrying on the rebellion and Henry III granted Leicester to his own younger son Edmund. His son Thomas repaired the castle and frequently resided there. Edward I came to stay in 1300, and Edward II in 1310 and 1311. The castle was also a favoured residence of Edward III's son John of Gaunt, who built the cellar surviving south of the hall. Richard II visited his uncle's castle in 1390 and it became royal when Gaunt's son Henry took the throne in 1399. During the early part of the minority of his grandson Henry VI the castle precinct was given a new southern boundary wall beyond the motte, together with a gateway to give access towards a newly added southern outer enclosure known as the Newark. As with many castles in county towns the later history of the castle is one of maintenance of the hall as a courthouse but the neglect of almost everything else. The castle played no role in the siege and capture of Leicester by Charles I in 1645.

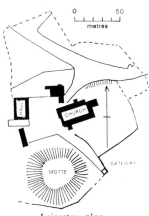

Leicester: plan

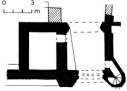

Gatehouse at Leicester   *Gatehouse at Leicester*

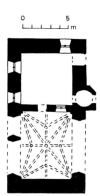

*Magazine Gateway
at Leicester*

Magazine Gateway at Leicester

A detailed description of the large parish church of St Mary de Castro belongs more to a book about Leicestershire churches. Originally cruciform and aisle-less, it was given a north aisle c1160, whilst the wide south aisle is a late 13th century rebuilding. The spire was rebuilt in 1783 and much of the exterior of the church, with several large late medieval windows, was restored in the 1850s. The courtyard west of the church is reached through a timber-framed gateway of 1445-59 beside the north aisle of the church. South of the courtyard is the motte, now 9m high but originally higher. Early 15th century walls bound the south and east sides of the base of the motte and in the angle between them is a ruined gatehouse. It measures 10m by 6.5m, and has a guardroom flanking the west side of a passage with four-centred archways, the outermost of which has a portcullis groove. A spiral stair in the polygonal turret on the SE corner led to an upper room.

The Court House west of the castle yard is the much altered mid 12th century hall given a new east facade of the 1690s. The hall measured 24m by 15m and had timber arcades of six bays, of which one capital is preserved. The roof structure is thought to be as old as the hall, a rare survival. The great chamber lay north of the hall, and the kitchen and service rooms lay to the south, and beyond is a 14th century vaulted cellar. Nothing remains of the 12th century inner bailey curtain wall although an excavation in 1939 found traces of its collapsed remains with a 12m wide ditch in front. A section survives of the more modest wall of the outer bailey to the south. SE of the castle, and now stranded in the middle of a busy ringroad roundabout, is the 15th century Magazine Gateway, which was the outer gateway of the southern extension of the castle known as the Newark. It measures 16.5m by 8.6m over walls 1.5m thick and contains a rib-vaulted passage so wide that on the east side there are separate arches for carts and pedestrians. The upper rooms are reached by a staircase in a domed polygonal turret on the west side. The square-headed two-light windows are mostly restorations of the 1890s. There are no remains of the town walls although excavations have traced them in a few places.

MELTON MOWBRAY CASTLE   SK 748188

SW of the bridge over the Eye is a small mound of the castle of the Mowbray family.

Earthworks at Sauvey

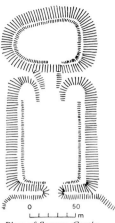

Plan of Sauvey Castle

0   50
⊢_⊥_⊥_⊥_⊣ m

MOUNTSORREL CASTLE   SK 585149   F

Under the terms of a treaty made between 1148 and 1153 the Earl of Leicester was to hold the castle at Mountsorrel as a tenant of the Earl of Leicester. The castle was surrendered to Henry II in 1174. The "tower over the well", the hall and the chamber are mentioned c1190, when Richard I had them repaired. After King John granted the lands of the earldom of Leicester to Saher de Quency, Earl of Winchester, he retained this castle in his own hands, until obliged under the terms of Magna Carta to hand it over to de Quency in 1215. Earlier in that year the king had ordered timber for making hoardings for the walls. The castle withstood a siege by Henry III's forces in 1217 and was relieved by de Quency, but his garrison deserted it after the royalist victory at Lincoln, and the castle was then destroyed by the Earl of Chester. The site is a rocky outcrop now surmounted by a monument. It commands a wide view to the east and has traces of entrenchments on the SW slope.

Earthworks at Whitwick

RATCLIFFE CULEY MOTTE   SP 328994

The Victoria County History describes this as a motte about 4m high, although Cathcart-King calls it a homestead moat on a sloping site.

SAPCOTE CASTLE   SP 488933

There are slight remains of a probable motte and bailey known as Toot Hill.

SAUVEY CASTLE   SK 787053

King John spent over £440 on fortifying this castle in 1211, although the impressive earthworks may go back to the 1140s. It was entrusted to William de Fors, Count of Aumale but had to be recovered forcibly when he rebelled in 1220, after which £30 was spent by the Sheriff of Leicestershire on repairing the palisades and buildings. In 1244 Henry III ordered the construction of a new chapel of wood with a roof of slates from a stable that had fallen down. Repairs were executed on two occasions during the 1250s but the site was plundered for materials during Edward I's reign and the keeper of the Forest of Rutland removed stone from it in 1373. The castle had a curtain wall around an inner ward about 70m by 40m, and a barbican towards an outer ward 70m wide extending 120m to the west, which probably only had a palisade. Streams on either side of the ridge were dammed to form a lake extending round the north, east and south sides to provide a strong outer defence. The lake, now drained, fed 10m wide wet moats on the exposed west side of each ward. The inner ward rampart rose 15m above this moat.

SCRAPTOFT MOTTE   SK 654059

A small mound with a depressed summit lies east of the village.

SHACKERSTONE CASTLE   SK 375069

North of the church is a mound 6m high with a ditch and counterscarp on the south and traces of a bailey on the SW. It is likely there were other outworks to the north.

SHAWELL MOTTE   SP 541796

This motte may be the site of the castle of Catthorpe, left unfinished in 1218 after Henry III prevented completion because he had not granted permission for it.

WHITWICK CASTLE   SK 436162   V

A mostly natural promontory in the middle of the village forms a 6m high platform about 100m long by 40m wide, although the northern end, on which is a 19th century house, lies at a lower level. The small mound hidden under vegetation in the middle of site is probably the buried base of a keep or tower house. A treaty of c1148-53 between the earls of Chester and Leicester mentions this site as yet to be fortified whilst another castle nearby at Ravenstone was to be destroyed. There is a mention of the castle, which belonged to the earls of Leicester, in 1204, and it was destroyed in 1217 by the Earl of Pembroke, because the then owner, Saher de Quency, was in rebellion. Henry de Beaumont was licensed to crenellate his house here by Edward II in 1320, and it later passed to the Hastings family.

GAZETTEER OF LINCOLNSHIRE CASTLES

BARROW-UPON-HUMBER   TA 064225

Beside a stream called the Beck at Barrow Haven, 1.2km NNW of the parish church is a large but low motte with two spacious baileys, originally protected by water-filled moats. There were once two other large outer enclosures. This may have been the castle of Peter of Goxhill mentioned by the Earl of Lincoln in a charter of the 1140s.

BARTON-ON-HUMBER CASTLE

Nothing remains of a castle founded here by Gilbert de Gaunt in the 1140s.

BOLINGBROKE CASTLE   TF 349650   F

William de Roumare, Earl of Lincoln may have had a castle here in the 11th century, and he was succeeded by the Gaunt family, but the present remains, revealed by excavation from 1965 onwards, represent a very fine stone fortress begun by Ranulph de Blundeville, Earl of Chester probably a few years after he was granted the additional title of Earl of Lincoln in 1217. On his death in 1232 the castle passed to his sister Hawise, and then reverted to the Crown, but it eventually passed, as did the earldom of Lincoln, to John de Lacy, who was married to a niece of de Blundeville. John's son Henry entertained Edward I within the castle in 1292. Henry's only son drowned in the well of his other fine castle at Denbigh and so Bolingbroke passed to his daughter Alice, who was married to Thomas, Earl of Lancaster.

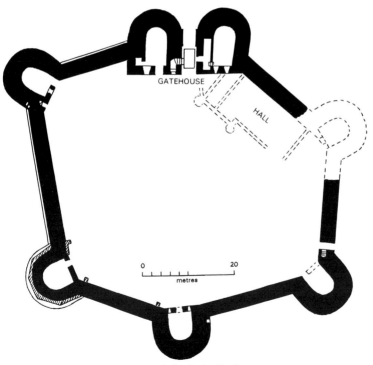

Plan of Bolingbroke Castle

Bolingbroke Castle

After Earl Thomas was executed for rebellion against Edward II in 1322 Alice held the castle until she died in 1348. Described in 1335 as weak and ruinous for lack of maintenance, the castle passed to Thomas's younger brother Henry, whose daughter Blanche married Edward III's son John of Gaunt, Duke of Lancaster. Their son Henry, born in the castle in 1367, was banished by his cousin Richard II in 1398 after quarrelling with Thomas Mowbray and challenging him to a fight. The king then disinherited Henry, but in 1399 the earl returned to claim back his estates, and ended up taking Richard's throne to become king himself as Henry IV. The castle has been part of the Duchy of Lancaster ever since. Part of the curtain wall collapsed in 1559 but the damage must have been at least partly made good since the castle was held in the Civil War for King Charles and was besieged by the Earl of Manchester in the autumn of 1643. The garrison seem to have abandoned it after the defeat at Winceby of a Royalist force sent out to relieve it. The castle had been dismantled by the time the estate was sold in 1650. Parts of the three southern towers still stood up high in the early 18th century, but the last high standing fragment collapsed in 1815.

The castle had a hexagonal court 60m by 50m enclosed by a curtain wall up to 3.4m thick above a plinth, and now standing up to 3m high. There are U-shaped towers 12m in diameter at five of the corners and a twin-towered gatehouse on the north side. When the walls were complete and fronted by a wet moat this would have been a very formidable castle. The towers at the NW and SW corners each have a wall about 1m thick facing the court with a doorway and single window. The similar wall in the Kitchen Tower at the south corner has two smaller windows set either side of a central doorway. No such wall survives in the SE tower and very little remains of the NE tower. None of the towers had loops facing the field at basement level. Each probably had two upper storeys but there is a dearth of staircases in the remains apart from a straight stair up from the jamb of a postern in the east wall beside the Auditor's Tower at the SE corner, and a stair leading down to the turning-bridge pit under the gatehouse entrance passage. The King's Tower at the SW corner was refaced externally as a polygon in 1451, probably to single it out as containing the principal private chambers. It is assumed that there were lean-to buildings against all the walls, but the only traces of them are foundations of a hall 9m wide and about 20m long, probably of later date, between the gatehouse and the NE tower, and traces of a later brick fireplace just west of the SE tower. The embanked and moated platform south of the castle may be a 15th century garden feature, unless it is a relic of an older castle, although it is more likely that an earlier castle stood on a hillock 0.2km north of the church, where 11th and 12th century pottery has been found.

Boothby Pagnell Manor

BOOTHBY PAGNELL MANOR   TF 970308

This is an unusually well preserved manor house of c1200 defended only by a moat, lying the grounds of the hall of 1824. It measures 17.4m by 8m and contains a hall over a rib-vaulted basement with walls 1.2m thick, and a solar at the north end over a tunnel-vaulted cellar. The hall has a fine fireplace in the west wall and had windows in the west, south and east walls. The two-light east window with a polygonal column and round arches cut unto a solid tympanum has been moved to a location in the south wall between a similar window and the doorway reached by external steps at the SE corner, and the existing four-light east window is of c1500. The solar has an east window with seats in the embrasure, like those in the hall, and traces of a possible second facing north. The southern end of the hall is now partitioned off to create two rooms. The wing on the west side and the existing roof and gables are not ancient. Built by the de Boothby family, the house passed in 1309 to the Pagnells.

BOURNE CASTLE   TF 093200   F

This was once an important castle with a stone keep with square angle turrets and a gatehouse with a round-arched portal between circular towers, but only damaged earthworks and parts of the moats remain in a public park. The outer bailey almost surrounded an inner bailey about 100m across with a keep at its southern end. Although a small excavation found no pottery earlier than the mid-13th century, the castle was the seat of a barony created for the de Rollos family in the early 12th century by Henry I. It passed to Baldwin de Clare and then went to the Wake family. Hugh Wake is said to have entertained his wife's cousin Edward III at the castle in 1330. It later passed to the Holland earls of Kent. Sir John Thimbleby, a leader of the Pilgrimage of Grace of 1536, lived at Bourne but according to Leland only earthworks then remained of the castle.

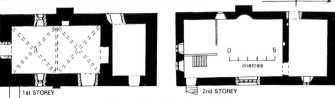

Plans of Boothby Pagnell Manor

CASTLE BYTHAM SK 991185 V

On a promontory within a loop of a stream NE of the village of Little Bytham is a high platform which once had a stone curtain wall, since there is a record of foundations and a round-headed arch being revealed in 1870. A counterscarp bank surrounds the ringwork on all sides except to the north, where there was a D-shaped barbican defending the approach from the L-shaped outer bailey lying to the east and north. There are signs that this bailey also had a stone curtain flanked by round towers. A reference in Domesday Book implies the existence of a castle here by 1085, when the manor was held by the Drogo de la Beuvriere, Lord of Holderness. He returned to Flanders shortly afterwards and Bytham was then granted to Odo, Count of Aumale, who was married to the king's sister Adelaide. Their descendant William le Gros, Count of Aumale, was made Earl of Yorkshire by King Stephen. His daughter and heiress, Hawise, married firstly William de Mandeville, Earl of Essex, who granted a tenancy of the castle to William de Coleville. In 1216 King John captured the castle from the rebellious William de Coleville and placed it in the custody of Hawise's second husband, William de Forz. After William de Coleville made his peace with the regents for the young Henry III the castle was ordered to be restored to him. However de Forz refused to hand it over and eventually broke out into open rebellion. In 1221 the castle was captured after a siege of a few days during which miners were employed against it. It seems that the defences may have then been dismantled. Whatever the case, the Colevilles were allowed to continue to occupy it, this time holding the manor directly from the king. A charter of 1226 mentions the chapel of "St Mary in the castle" and another chapel of "St Thomas the Martyr in the barbican". The castle passed to the Bassets in 1369 and in the 1390s was owned by Joan, Countess of Hereford, mother of the future Henry IV, whose grandchildren then living with her at Bytham included the future Henry V. The castle was a ruin when seen by Leland c1540, it then being owned by John Russell since the attainder of Lord Hussey in 1537 for his part in the Pilgrimage of Grace. See pages 7 & 48.

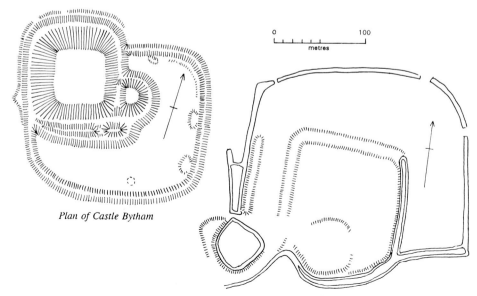

0   100
metres

Plan of Castle Bytham

Plan of Bourne Castle

Castle Bytham

CASTLE CARLTON   TF 396837   V

In 1219 the Earl of Salisbury was ordered not to strengthen this castle, which is said to have been built in Henry I's reign by Sir Hugh Bardolph. A motte, unusually high for Lincolnshire, and two baileys west of it lie in woodland 3km ESE of Legbourne.

CORBY CASTLE   TF 000252   V

A motte rising about 4m high to a summit 30m across lies NW of the church.

ERESBY MANOR   TF 394652

Excavations in 1968 found footings of the NW tower and an adjacent curtain wall of the castle which Edward I licensed John, Lord Bek to crenellate in 1276. His daughter's son was created Lord Willoughby de Eresby. Effigies of the first three lords and a brass of William, 5th Lord, lie in a chapel in nearby Spilsby parish church. The excavations also found parts of the kitchen, remodelled in brick by Robert, 6th Lord Willoughby, who was married to a daughter of Ralph, Lord Cromwell. After his marriage to Katherine Willoughby in 1533 Charles Brandon, Duke of Suffolk built a new H-planned house nearby to the SE. Only a converted stableblock remains.

FLEET CASTLE   TF 385232

Little now remains of a motte 0.3km SE of Fleet Church. Pottery of the late 11th and 12th centuries was found in an excavation in 1913.

FOLKINGHAM CASTLE   TF 074335   V

A strong moated platform with a counterscarp bank on the east and an outer enclosure to the north is all that remains of the castle which Edward II licensed Henry de Beaumont to crenellate in 1312, Edward I having earlier granted the manor to him. The north enclosure and perhaps also the much larger outer enclosure extending down to the stream on the east may go back to the period when the Gaunt family had their chief seat here. The castle buildings were ruinous when seen by Leland c1540. The site is occupied by a the gateway of a house of correction dated 1825 and replacing an older prison built here in 1611. The prison was closed in 1878 and the other buildings were demolished in 1955, but the gateway remains in use as one of the Landmark Trust's holiday homes.

FRAMPTON CASTLE   TF 327391

The slight traces of a square moated platform SE of the church may be relics of the castle mentioned in 1216.

GAINSBOROUGH CASTLE   TF 044227

Within woodland at Thonock on the edge of a west facing escarpment north of the town is a ringwork 5m high and 50m by 60m across with a counterscarp bank beyond its ditch on the south and a D-shaped bailey 90m by 80m to the north. An outer bailey with a diameter of 160m protecting the east and south sides of the motte is thought to be a later addition. This castle was either erected by Roger de Poitou, who held the estate at the time of Domesday Book in 1086, or by his successor the Count of Mortain. Edward I's brother Edmund, Earl of Cornwall had a residence here as part of the Honour of Lancaster and it is likely there were stone buildings. It remained in use until the 15th century but had evidently been long abandoned by c1540 when Leland described the site as "a great motid manor place".

GAINSBOROUGH OLD HALL   SK 814902   O

There is some doubt as to how much damage was done to this building by the Lancastrians in 1470 and consequently there is uncertainly as to how much of the building dates from just after the marriage of Thomas Burgh and Margaret Roos in c1464, and how much is a rebuilding of the 1470s. The north range containing the hall and solar is a splendid timber-framed structure, but the oriel at the hall NE corner is of ashlar and the east wing east wall, the huge kitchen projecting at the NW corner, and the lofty octagonal tower at the NE corner are of brick with stone dressings. The embattled tower may have been added as a status symbol lookout after Thomas was made a lord by Henry VII in 1487. It is 6m in diameter over walls 0.7m thick and contains three storeys of private rooms connected by a staircase in a polygonal turret rising above the main building on the south side, and having latrines furnished with crossloops in a second turret on the east. There was probably a gatehouse in the vanished south range. After the death of Thomas, 5th Lord Burgh in 1596 the hall was sold to the London merchant William Hickman, who built the west range. His son Willoughby was created Baron Gainsborough in 1643. The Hickmans later moved to Thonock and Gainsborough Old Hall became a linen factory. It is now a monument managed jointly by the county council and English Heritage.

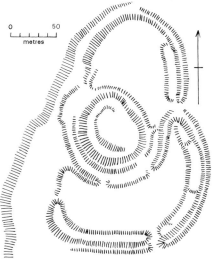

0   50
metres

Plan of Gainsborough Castle

Gainsborough Old Hall

GOLTHO CASTLE   TF 116774

Excavation of an earthwork to the south of the brick church of c1640 revealed a site with remarkable history. In the late 11th century the earthworks of an enclosure of c850 were remodelled into a tiny motte and bailey castle. The bailey was about 40m square with rounded corners and had the motte in the NE corner. In the middle of the bailey was an aisled timber hall about 15m long by 7m wide, and there was a gatehouse on the east side. Traces of a wooden tower about 3m square were found in the base of the motte, the upper part of the motte having been levelled in the mid 12th century and the material used to widen the bailey rampart internally.

GRIMSBY CASTLE

In 1200 King John allocated £80 for the construction of a stronghold here. Not much of the money was spent upon the project before it was abandoned, and in 1214 the accumulated stocks of stone and lime for it were sold.

Gainsborough Old Hall

GRIMSTHORPE CASTLE   TF 044227   O

The only relic of the medieval castle is King John's Tower, a three storey structure 9m by 7.5m over walls 2m thick, projecting boldly from the east side of the 16th century building. Grimsthorpe belonged to Gilbert de Gaunt in the late 13th century but the tower, which contains rib-vaulted rooms with later windows and has 19th century battlements, is more likely to be the work of Henry de Beaumont in the early 14th century. It is said to have been one of four towers set at the corners of a building with four ranges. Leland mentions a gatehouse and ditch and says that an outer court had recently been added. This outer court was the work of Charles Brandon, Duke of Suffolk, and was completed shortly before a visit by Henry VIII. The Duke had obtained Grimsthorpe by marrying the daughter of William, 10th Lord Willoughby, to whom the estates formerly belonging to Lord Beaumont had been granted in 1507, and seems to have rebuilt almost the whole structure, providing new state rooms in the east range. A new show-front on the north side was built by Robert, 3rd Earl of Lindsey in the 1680s. It contains a large entrance hall, which was remodelled to a design by Sir John Vanbrugh in the 1720s for the Duke of Ancaster, but which may perhaps represent the original medieval great hall. The bay windows on the east side seem to have been added in the late 18th century. The Tudor style work on the west side was built for Lord Gwydir in the early 19th century. His descendants, created earls of Ancaster in 1892, are still in possession.

Grimsthorpe Castle

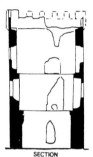

SECTION

HEYDOUR: CASTLE HILLS   TF 007397

The ringwork not far west of the church looks as if it has buried remains of a curtain wall. The ditch was once water filled and there is a surrounding bailey.

HOUGH ON THE HILL CASTLE   SK 924465

A damaged motte east of the church had a good view to the NW.

HUSSEY TOWER   TF 333436   V

A brick solar tower built by Richard Benington in the mid 15th century lies not far to the SE of the centre of Boston. Benington was a justice of the peace for the Holland district and a collector of customs at Boston. His tower measures 9.2m by 8.3m over walls which are 1.4m thick in the basement (which was once rib-vaulted), but progressively thinner in the upper two storeys. These levels have fireplaces in the west end wall and two-light windows of stone facing north and south. The presence of a second fireplace in the east wall suggests the second storey room was subdivided. The basement has a fireplace in the north wall, two blocked loops facing south and the entrance doorway in the east wall, facing towards a hall block which was demolished in 1725. The second storey also had a doorway from the hall block (now blocked, like the windows), whilst the third storey doorway probably gave access to the hall roof. All the levels are connected by a spiral stair in an octagonal turret at the NE corner. The steps are carried on radiating brick arches. What remains of the parapet projects out slightly on a moulded course and has a polygonal tourelle at the SW corner. The tower and hall were accompanied by a gatehouse (dismantled by 1565), a stable, bakehouse, and a mill.

3rd STOREY

0   5
metres

2nd STOREY

1st STOREY

Hussey Tower: plans

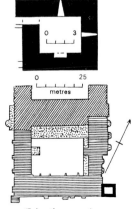

Grimsthorpe: plans

The East Gate of Lincoln Castle

Hussey Tower

Lincoln: plan of Pottergate

KINGERBY MANOR   TF 057928

Surrounding the house built in 1812 by James Young is a moat, still water filled on the north site of a house or castle burnt in 1216 by King John.

LEGSBY MOTTE   TF 133839

This small motte has a summit 12m by 9m and a surrounding ditch 1m deep.

The Pottergate at Lincoln

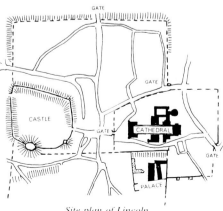

Site plan of Lincoln

LINCOLN BISHOP'S PALACE   SK 978719   E

In 1285 Edward I granted Bishop Sutton a licence for the cathedral close in the SE corner of the walled city to be provided with embattled walls and gates, Two thirds of the circuit formed part of the city defences, for the cathedral east end overlies the line of the original Roman east wall and new wall was needed beyond it. Two 14th century gateways remain, the impressive three storey Exchequer Gate west of the cathedral and the Potter Gate to the east. The best preserved sections of the precinct wall are on the SE, where amongst the gardens there are remains of four embattled towers, probably those built under the terms of a second crenellation licence of 1319 to Bishop Dalderby, and on the south side, where the wall-walk still remains.

On a shelf below the south wall of the precinct, and thus not separately defensible, lies the bishop's palace, for which another crenellation licence was granted to Bishop Burghersh in 1329 by Edward III. The oldest part of the palace is a vaulted undercroft built by Bishop St Hugh in the late 12th century, above which was his private hall, with a chamber commanding a fine view at the south end, where a wing projects to the east. The court between the private hall and the aisled public hall to the west narrows to a corridor blocked by an embattled porch-tower built by Bishop Alnwick in the 1430s. This part and the wing SE of it of the same date, which contained a chapel, are the only parts still roofed. The western hall for public use is early 13th century, begun by St Hugh, but completed in the 1230s by Hugh of Wells. It measures 31.5m long by 21m wide and has an original SW porch and a 15th century NW oriel window. At the south end three doorways lead under where there is now an upper chapel of 1898 to a passage flanked by a buttery and pantry through to a kitchen beyond. To the south is a terraced garden enclosed on the east by a 3m thick and 4.5m section of the wall of the Late Roman suburb below the old town.

Lincoln Bishop's Palace: service doorways

Alnwick's Tower at Lincoln Bishop's Palace

LINCOLN CASTLE   SK 975719   O

During his campaign in Lincolnshire in 1068 William I ordered the construction of a castle in the SW corner of the original Roman walled town, the exceptional number of 166 houses being destroyed to make room for it. During the 1070s a new cathedral was built in the SE corner of the Roman town as part of the Norman re-organisation of the church requiring cathedrals to be in walled towns. The bishop of Lincoln owed the service of 20 knights for the castle garrison, and another 16 were owed by the family that eventually took the surname of Haye, but in the 1120s Bishop Alexander was allowed by Henry I to transfer the service of his knights to the castle he was then building at Newark. The shell keep at Lincoln is named the Lucy Tower after the wife of Ivo Taillbois (or Tallboys), who is thought to have been the sheriff of Lincoln during Henry I's reign, apparently in succession to Thorold, who seems to have been Lucy's father. Thus arose the claim by Lucy's descendants to the the offices of sheriff of Lincoln and keeper of Lincoln Castle.

In 1140 the city and castle were seized by the Empress Matilda. Although King Stephen soon recovered them, in December that year the castle keep was occupied by William de Roumare, son of Lucy by her second husband Roger Fitzgerald, and his half-brother Ranulph les Gernons, Earl of Chester, whose father had been Lucy's third husband. When Stephen besieged the castle Ranulph managed to escape from the beleaguered fortress and bring up reinforcements under Matilda's half brother, Robert, Earl of Gloucester. They defeated King Stephen in a battle outside the city and the king was taken prisoner. He was only released when forces loyal to him captured Earl Robert and an exchange of prisoners was made in September 1141. The king agreed on terms with Ranulph les Gernons and William de Roumare, and the latter was created Earl of Lincoln. Stephen failed to capture the castle during another campaign in 1144, during which there was an abortive attempt to built a siegework nearby, but in 1146 he captured Ranulph and forced him to surrender his castles, including Lincoln. Stephen stayed in the castle that Christmas and wore his crown in defiance of a superstition forbidding a sovereign to do so in the city. In 1149 Stephen allowed Ranulph to fortify a tower in the castle until the king was able to hand over to him the castle of Tickhill in exchange, and it appears that the second motte upon which the Observatory Tower now stands was added about this time.

The West Gate at Lincoln

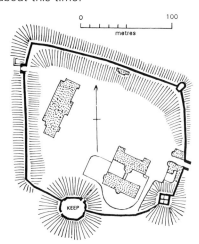

Plan of Lincoln Castle

Cobb Hall at Lincoln   *The West Gate at Lincoln*

When Henry II came to the throne in 1154 he confirmed Richard de la Haye as constable of the castle. In 1191 the castle was held by Nichola de la Haye for Prince John against a siege by Richard I's chancellor, William de Longchamp. The elderly Nichola held the castle for King John in 1216 against an attack by Gilbert de Gaunt and Robert de Ropsley. They retired when John advanced to its relief but made another attempt upon after his death in October at Newark. In May 1217 another royalist force led by the Earls of Pembroke and Chester advanced to its relief. The attackers were caught in a pincer movement between a sally by the garrison and the relief army and were defeated in a second battle of Lincoln commonly known as "Lincoln Fair". Afterwards the Earl of Chester, Ranulph de Blundeville, who was a descendant of Lucy, was given the additional title of Earl of Lincoln. The earldom and the constableship of the castle eventually both passed to Henry de Lacy, and then via his daughter Alice to the duchy of Lancaster, which has been merged with the crown since the accession of Henry IV in 1399. The east gateway was remodelled in the 1220s and the west gate was rebuilt in the 1230s at a cost of £54. The chapel was repaired in 1269 and some time during the second half of the 13th century the round Tower known as Cobb Hall was added at the NE corner.

By 1327 the castle was in a very decayed state, needing £1000 worth of repairs. It was no longer needed as either a fortress or residence and basically served just to provide a courthouse and prison for the county. However, there must have been some 14th century rebuilding, since much of the Observatory Tower is of that period. During the Civil War the castle was held by the Royalists until in May 1644 it was stormed by a Parliamentary force under Lord Manchester, despite the attackers' scaling ladders proving to be too short, and the fact that the garrison numbered 650 men, which should have been adequate for its defence. The castle was then probably demilitarised but the outer walls were left intact for the safe keeping of prisoners. In 1831 the county magistrates purchased the castle from the Duchy of Lancaster. The courthouse erected in 1826 still retains that purpose but the castle ceased to hold prisoners in 1878, and the prison now serves as the county records office.

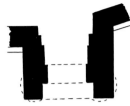

Plan of East Gate

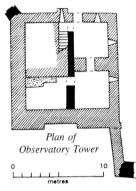

*Plan of
Observatory Tower*

0   10
└─┴─┴─┴─┴─┴─┴─┴─┴─┴─┘
        metres

Plan of Cobb Hall

Lincoln Castle has a bailey 170m long from east to west by 150m wide, the north and west walls being nearly straight and lying on unusually wide and high ramparts. Such a large bailey is quite exceptional for the main enclosure of an English castle but here there was no outer bailey as would be normal for such an important castle. The motte on the south side bearing the shell keep known as the Lucy Tower is original 11th century work. Excavations have shown that the second motte in the SE corner is probably a mid 12th century addition, raised coeval with the base of a tower about 12m square. Above the buried foundations most of it was rebuilt in the 14th century but the east-west crosswall is original with one archway. The tower was again remodelled in the early 19th century and upon the SW of it (the only part not open to the sky), the then governor of the prison added a round turret, supposedly as a prison-guards lookout, but really for astronomical purposes, from which the building takes its present name of the Observatory Tower.

The 12th century shell keep on the other mound is an irregular polygon about 25m by 20m within a wall 1.9m thick, in which are wide internal recesses at the east and west ends. Most of the external corners have pilaster buttresses and where the curtain wall against the shell wall it is continued up in the form of small turrets to the same height (about 6m) as the shell wall. A round arched entrance with a billet and scallop motif on the hood-mould lies in a projection facing NE and is approached by a long flight of steps. There is a postern doorway with a drawbar slot facing SW, outside the curtain wall. The interior was used as the prison burial ground in the mid 19th century. At one time there would have been lean-to wooden-framed lodgings, and before that a timber-framed tower named after Countess Lucy, the name later being transferred to the well-preserved surrounding shell-wall.

The east side of Lincoln Castle

The Lucy Tower at Lincoln

The curtain wall of the bailey is one of the most impressive and complete of its date and type in the whole of Britain. Although it has been much repaired over the years, especially in its upper parts, the wall still has sections of herringbone masonry making it likely that the whole of the circuit and the two gateways had been completed by the 1120s. Although the section between the mottes is not accessible, visitors can explore the wall-walk all the way round the rest of the circuit, where the wall is up to 8m high and 2.2m thick and stands on a bank up to 9m high. Only Carisbrooke in the Isle of Wight has a similarly well-preserved (and equally publicly accessible) curtain wall of such an early period. The two gateways and the tower at the NE corner provided some means of flanking fire, but nevertheless the wall was less than adequately flanked by later medieval standards, hence its vulnerability to a storming party during the Civil War siege in spite of its considerable height.

The West Gate lies just to the south of the Roman west gate, the base of which was discovered in 1836. It is a square projection having just one room over a passage with a plain round-arched portal with a portcullis groove that was only reopened a few years ago. On the north side of the approach to the gate are remains of a later barbican. The gateway is said to have been built c1110-15 to allow Bishop Robert Bloet access through the bailey to the cathedral from the original episcopal palace lying further west. If the portcullis groove is original it is one of the earliest in Britain. The 10m wide East Gate is thought to have been damaged in the siege of 1217, in consequence of which a new outer pointed arch was added with a pair of round bartizans above. The tiny doorways in the outer parts of these bartizans led to the wall-walk of a barbican added in front of the gateway but removed in 1791. The oriel window overhanging the north side of the entrance passage was brought in from another building in 1849. These gateways and NE corner tower known as Cobb Hall now all stand to the same height as the curtain wall-walk but must originally been higher. Cobb Hall measures 8.2m in diameter over walls 2.1m thick pierced with wide embrasures for arrow-loops on each of two rib-vaulted storeys. A straight stair on the west side leads from the entrance doorway to the wall-walk.

On the north side of the city a Roman gateway known as the Newport Arch still survives. Traces of the Roman city walls remain further east of it, and the base of the northern U-shaped tower of the Roman East Gate also lie exposed. The enclosed area soon proved inadequate to contain the thriving town and a suburb on the steep slope to the south was also walled in Roman times, one portion remaining by the bishop's palace. The castle and cathedral between them took up almost all the southern half of the area of the original walled town. The medieval extensions of the defences to include the bishop's palace and the cathedral close projecting beyond the line of the Roman walls have already been described (see page 53).

MOULTON CASTLE   TF 313214

An oval moated platform probably marks the site of the castle held by Thomas de Moulton in 1217. Possibly from this site have come the round turrets beside the north porch of Holbeach church.

OWSTON CASTLE   SE 806003   F

Roger de Mowbray's castle in the Isle of Axholm was probably destroyed after the failure of his rebellion against William II in 1095 since it is not included in a list of his castles in the possession of Henry I in 1130. It was refortified during the rebellion of 1173-4 but was captured for Henry II by his kinsman Geoffrey Plantagenet, Bishop-elect of Lincoln. It was ordered to be destroyed and in 1180 Adam Painel was fined for not carrying this out thoroughly enough. This may explain the present damaged condition of the motte. The church just to the north may occupy the bailey.

ROCHFORD TOWER   TF 351444

The Rochford family had a moated house here before they built this brick tower house in the late 15th century. Measuring 8.4m by 7.9m over walls up to 1.4m thick, It is similar to the slightly larger Hussey Tower nearby. Although derelict it is better preserved than the other tower (there was once a third tower of this type further east at Butterwick) and differs in having brick surrounds to the windows, an extra fourth storey and a parapet carried on a corbel table of trefoil arches. There are octagonal bartizans at three of the corners, the SE corner having a spiral stair in an octagonal turret. The lowest two levels have doorways (the upper one blocked) to a former narrow block that linked the tower to a hall block demolished in 1807. The brick-vaulted lowest level is subdivided and the eastern part has its own entrance doorway, which is fitted with a drawbar slot. A third doorway leads onto the foot of the staircase, which does not communicate with the basement. The room above has three-light windows with wooden mullions facing east and west and a fireplace in the south wall. The upper storeys have smaller windows. There are no latrines.

2nd STOREY

0   5
L__I__I__I__I__I m

1st STOREY

Rochford Tower   *Rochford: plans*   *Rochford Tower*

The last remains of Sleaford Castle

SCRIVELSBY COURT   TF 270660

Most of the house of the Dymocke family has been demolished. Still remaining is a wet moat on the south side and an office range containing a blocked gateway and a medieval window with ogee-headed lights. The range bears the date 1574 and contains much 18th century work. The Dymockes inherited the estate from the Marmions in the mid 14th century, and with it the office of Royal Champion. The Lion Gate at the entrance to the deer park has old parts but was rebuilt in 1833.

SLEAFORD CASTLE   TF 065455   F

This castle was built by Alexander, Bishop of Lincoln during the 1120s and 30s. It was taken by King Stephen in 1139, more by bribery than force of arms, and in 1221 was attacked by the rebel William de Fors, Count of Aumale. The castle was "very well mantayned" when visited by Leland but it was stripped of its roof after being granted by Edward VI to the Duke of Somerset, and by 1720 only three fragments still stood. The castle consisted of inner and middle wards lying side-by-side on a square moated platform which itself lay in the NE corner of a square outer court, in the southern part of which lay a large barn. Of the walls all that remains is a tumbled fragment of one corner of the NE corner tower. There are thought to have been a tower keep at the NW corner of the inner ward, and towers at the other corners, with the inner gateway in the crosswall between the wards running south from it. In the garden of Old House is a 15th century shield of kneeling angels from the castle, and a number of 14th century fragments, including a king's head, a two-light window and a polygonal chimneystack with turret-pots, are built into the Manor House.

Moats at Sleaford Castle

South Kyme Tower   *Somerton Castle*

SOMERTON CASTLE   SK 954588

Anthony Bek, Bishop of Durham inherited the manor of Somerton from his mother Eva de Grey on her death in 1279. He soon began building a castle here, and obtained a licence to crenellate it from Edward I in 1281. For reasons that are unknown the bishop gifted the castle to Edward II in 1309. The king carried out some repairs in 1323-6, but when surveyed at the accession of Edward III in 1327 the castle was decayed because its lead roofs had been stolen. The castle was briefly leased to John de Roos and then in 1334 John Crabbe was made its constable in return for valuable service rendered at the siege of Berwick the previous year. The king stayed at the castle in the autumn of 1334 and during the next two years Crabbe spent £222 on repairs which included alterations to the moats and rebuilding the outer drawbridge. Further repairs were executed before King John of France was kept a prisoner in the castle from July 1359 until moved to Berkhamsted in March 1360. The French king had been captured during the battle of Poitiers in 1356. The timber-framed stables in the outer ward collapsed during a storm in 1372. Despite expenditure of about £10 upon maintenance the castle in 1392 was reported to need more than £100 spending on repairs to its walls, bridges, moats, roofs, glazing and ironwork.

In 1408 Henry IV granted a life interest in the castle to Sir Ralph Rochford, who spent over £112 on repairs during the next three years. In 1415 Rochford was persuaded to give up the castle in favour of Henry IV's brother, Thomas, Duke of Clarence. It was repaired by Henry V in 1422, not long after his uncle's death. Edward IV granted the castle to his brother George, Duke of Clarence, but it reverted to the Crown upon his attainder in 1478. Henry made Somerton part of the duchy of Lancaster. A survey of 1525 suggests that the building had by then been stripped of its wood, metal and other easily reusable parts, and in 1601 the ruins were said to be "utterley defaced and fallen almost downe to the ground."

The account of 1601 evidently exaggerated the condition of the castle to some degree for one tower still stands 14m high, and is complete except for the upper parts of the parapet. It measures about 9m in diameter and contains a vaulted basement and two upper storeys. Cross-shaped arrow loops survive at third storey level, one of them being in a turret adjoining on the west side. A late 16th century farmhouse with many more recent windows adjoins the tower, which stood at the SE corner of a quadrangular court 75m long from north to south by 60m wide. The vaulted basements of the SW and NE corner towers also remain, but hardly anything of the curtain walls, nor any sign of a gatehouse. The southern towers have dome-vaults but that in the NE tower has ribs radiating from a central pier. A small vaulted room adjoins the south side of this tower, which lies ruinous in an orchard. A wet moat up to 9m wide protecting the east and west sides extends 145m beyond the line of the former north wall to allow space for a garden, in which are two conjoined fish-ponds. A platform 85m wide and 140m long in front of the south side of the castle is enclosed by a second moat up to 25m long which extends alongside part of the inner moat on the east and west sides (where it is crossed by causeways), and has beyond it a high counterscarp bank. This outer moat may represent the works recorded on moats in the 1330s, perhaps with the intention of creating a tilt-yard.

SOUTH KYME TOWER   TF 168496   V

Sir Gilbert de Umfraville inherited the manor in 1338 and probably built this ashlar-faced embattled tower in the last fifteen years or so before his death in 1381. It measures 8.8m square over walls 1.5m thick above the plinth, and is 23m high to the top of the stair turret which projects from the south end of the east wall. The basement has an octopartite rib-vault with the de Umfraville arms on the central boss. Above are three upper storeys each with a two-light window in the middle of each side. Until dismantled in the 1720s a hall block lay to the south, where there are a row of joist-holes and doorways in the two lowest levels. There was also originally also a second tower. All these buildings lay within a wet moat. South Kyme passed to the Burdons and then in the 15th century went to the Tallboys family. It passed to Sir Edward Dymoke in 1530, and then in the early 18th century went to the Duke of Newcastle.

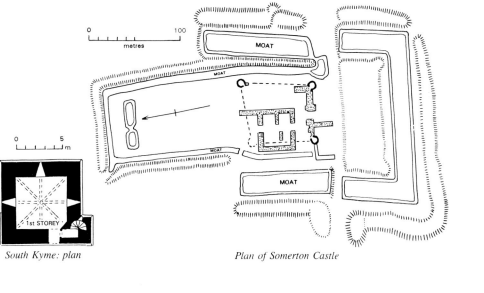

South Kyme: plan   *Plan of Somerton Castle*

The last tower of the town wall at Stamford

STAINBY MOTTE   SK 910227

Tower Hill to the south of the village appears to have been a small motte.

STAMFORD CASTLE   TF 028070   V

It is likely that the castle towards the SW end of the town on the north bank of the River Welland was founded by William I during his campaign in Lincolnshire in 1068. Turold, Abbot of Peterborough took refuge in the town from Hereward the Wake in 1070, and it appears that it already had a bank and ditch, although the fortified borough founded by Edward the Elder in 918 against the Danes had been on the south bank of the river. In 1153 Henry of Anjou captured the town fairly easily but the castle withstood all assaults and the garrison only surrendered when they gave up hope of King Stephen coming to their relief. The castle chapel is mentioned in 1199, and in 1216 King John gave William de Warenne lands at Uffington to pay for the sustinance of the garrison of his castle at Stamford. In 1218 and 1226 the young Henry III made timber available for the town defences, and 20 oaks were granted in 1224 for work upon the domestic buildings of the castle. They were repaired in 1256, when there is also a mention of a prison. About that time the town was provided with stone walls. In a survey of 1340 the decayed castle is reported as having "an old tower, a great hall, a chamber with a solar, a chapel, a turret and a house for a prison". The castle is said to have been finally demolished during Richard III's reign and the materials from it used to repair the Carmelite Friary.

The motte was removed in 1935 to build a car park (now a bus station). With it went the lower parts of a shell keep about 20m across internally, probably of the late 12th century when it appears that the motte was enlarged, with the result that its ditch was filled in. The motte lay entirely within the bailey and took up most of its space, and it is assumed that the gatehouse lay on the east, towards the town centre. On the west side the walls ran out to a salient angle. Excavations begun in 1971 revealed the lower parts of the domestic buildings overlying Saxon ditches in the SE corner. In the mid 12th century a hall about 14m long by 11m wide, aisled with arcades of three bays, was built over earlier structures containing ovens. A chamber block 16m long by 7m wide internally was added at the west end in the late 12th century and a block containing service rooms was provided at the east end. The chamber block had three loops in wide embrasures in the 2.2m thick south wall. In the early 13th century a porch opening into the chamber block was added in the re-entrant angle between it and the hall. After remodelling later in the 13th century the hall had just a north aisle and the usual arrangement of triple doorways (still standing) to various service rooms at the east end, and a court was walled off in front of the chamber block. The hall was in turn given a porch at its NE corner in the 14th century. The excavations also revealed a corner of a building thought to be a prison lying SW of the motte on the edge of its ditch. South of this was a building with a south-facing apse. A fragment of the bailey wall still stands on the NW side and on the south side a reset doorway survives amongst cottages in Bath Row.

The small round tower surviving at the NW corner of the town walls may be a 17th century rebuilding. Only small fragments remain of the rest of the circuit. South of the tower lay St Peter's Gate, on the north side were the St Clement's Gate and New Gate, and in the middle of the short NE end was the St Paul's Gate. The St George's Gate and the Water Gate faced SE, and the Bridge Gate faced south, the enclosed area being about 850m long with a greatest width of about 300m.

STOW CASTLE   SK 881820

A moat remains of a building for which a crenellation licence was granted in 1336.

SWINESHEAD CASTLE   TF 243410   F

This castle is mentioned in 1186, and in King John's reign. Beside a stream which probably filled the moats is a motte with a bailey in the form of a wide counterscarp bank.

Service doorways of the hall at Stamford   *Doorway at Stamford*

TATTERSHALL CASTLE   TF 576211   O

Tattershall was held by a Norman called Eudo at the time of Domesday Book in 1086. His descendants eventually took the name Tateshale, and there was then a sequence of them, all called Robert, the second of which was licensed by Henry III in 1231 to fortify his residence here. The result was a polygonal walled enclosure with a moat and several circular flanking towers. The estate then passed through various hands before passing to Ralph, Lord Cromwell with his marriage to Maud Bernack c1350. It was his grandson Ralph, 3rd Lord Cromwell, who rebuilt the castle and provided it with the huge brick tower dominating the countryside around as an expression of his power and wealth. From the building accounts which partly survive it appears that work on the tower began c1433 and continued for about fifteen years. The funds for building work upon both the castle and collegiate church at Tattershall and also at Wingfield in Derbyshire were obtained through his marriage to an heiress, Margaret Deincourt, and his possession of a number of lucrative offices, in particular the Treasurership of England during the second half of the minority of Henry VI.

After Lord Cromwell died in 1456 some of his estates were sold to pay for the completion of the college at Tattershall and the rest passed to his niece Joan and were forfeited to the Crown after her husband Humphrey Bourchier was killed at the battle of Barnet in 1471. Henry VII granted the castle to his mother Margaret Beaufort, Countess of Richmond, and Henry VIII granted it to Charles Brandon, Duke of Suffolk. The castle later went to Sir Henry Sidney, but he sold it to Lord Clinton, later Earl of Lincoln, and it remained with his descendants until it passed to the Fortescues in 1693. It was probably ruinous by then and is shown as roofless in an engraving of 1726 by the Buck brothers. In the 19th century the stone parts of the building were demolished for their materials. The chimney pieces in the tower had been removed for shipment abroad when Lord Curzon purchased the castle in 1911 but he managed to rescue and reinstate them. The tower was restored, its machicolated galleries rebuilt, and the moats cleared out again. The site was bequeathed to the National Trust in 1925.

Fireplace in the great tower at Tattershall

The base of the great tower at Tattershall

The 13th century castle had a polygonal court about 65m by 55m. Apart from the moat, which has a 15th century brick revetment on the outer bank for much of its circuit, the only remains are the foundations of two round towers about 7.5m in diameter set on either side of the tower house, plus a slight trace of a third on the south side. Their disposition suggest that there may have been three more single towers and the Buck engraving shows a pair of polygonal towers or turrets flanking the gateway on the NE side, along with fragments of the domestic buildings within the court. From this engraving we can infer that a hall aligned from north to south stood in front of the tower house, and that this hall had an oriel window lighting the east side of the dais at the north end, beyond which was a 17th century range set from east to west. The service rooms and kitchen must have been in the SW corner and a chapel with a chantry chapel on its northern side lay on the south side of the court. A narrower outer moat added in the 1430s around the east, north and west sides encloses two other L-shaped platforms. The eastern one formed the middle ward and has a truncated portion of a 15th century building now forming the ticket office and shop, and footings of another long range, whilst the other platform has the shell of a block 30m long containing stables with servants' quarters above. The Buck engraving shows a gatehouse standing at the west end of the middle ward. Originally the outer moat enclosed the south side as well, where there was a private garden.

The brick tower house measures 18.8m by 14.8m over walls which are 3.5m thick at second storey level, except that the east wall has the still greater thickness of 4.5m, although since it is filled with chambers and galleries very little of it is actually solid walling. At the corners are octagonal turrets 6m in diameter containing small extra rooms. Because of the way the tower was tucked in behind the older hall and space had to be left for a passage between the two buildings, the eastern turrets do not project as far from the east wall as the other turrets do on the west side. The tower would have been difficult to defend in isolation from the rest of the castle since it has three separate entrances from the courtyard. One leads directly onto the base of the spiral stair to the three upper storeys which formed a private suite for Lord Cromwell. The next leads down a steep set of steps into a low vaulted basement with a well, probably intended primarily for storage, and the third entrance leads into a fine living room, or parlour, at courtyard level, and without communication with the levels above or below. The basement only has narrow loops in the north and south end walls but the four levels above all have a pair of evenly spaced two-light windows of stone. The parlour additionally has a window in each end wall and a latrine in the SE corner, tucked under the foot of the staircase. This room has a particularly fine heraldic fireplace which backs onto a small room in the wall reached from the entrance passage. A similar room lies below it.

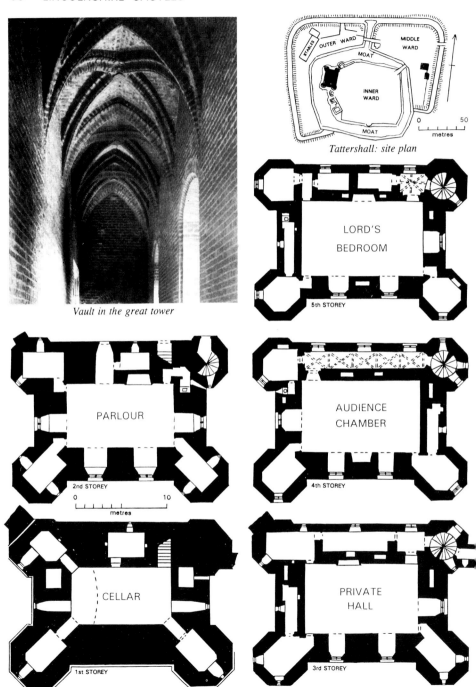

Vault in the great tower

Tattershall: site plan

LORD'S
BEDROOM

5th STOREY

PARLOUR

2nd STOREY

AUDIENCE
CHAMBER

4th STOREY

CELLAR

1st STOREY

PRIVATE
HALL

3rd STOREY

Plans of the great tower at Tattershall

Galleries on the great tower   _The great tower at Tattershall_

The third storey of the tower served as Lord Cromwell's private hall and has another fine fireplace and a latrine reached from the room in the NW turret. The east wall has two doorways, arranged so that one could enter the hall either from the lobby next the staircase, or by going through two other chambers, the second of them in the NE turret, before reaching the other doorway. The fourth storey was the audience chamber in which the lord would sit on a canopied seat at the south end of the room. Those waiting to see him went from the staircase along a gallery with a rib-vault of moulded brick to a doorway at the NE corner of the main room. The NE turret contains a waiting room with a fireplace and latrine, whilst the lord had his own latrine reached from the room in the SW turret. The fifth storey contained the lord's bedroom, his canopied bed being set against the north end wall, and accordingly the entrance from the stair is here at the SE corner, from a square lobby with another brick rib-vault. The rooms in the western turrets at this level have fireplaces and the NW one has a latrine. The NE turret room was probably a study, and the room south of it was perhaps a treasury, being in the most secure and private place in the castle. At the summit are machicolated galleries carrying wall-walks above them, the parapets being mostly restoration work. The machicolations do command all three entrances but it is clear that they exist more for visual effect than to allow a vigorous defence. The turrets have rooms at both levels, the uppermost rooms each having a pair of cross-loops facing the field and trap-doors to give access to their roofs, which are now much flatter than the spire-like roofs shown in the Buck engraving. The parapets of the turrets are carried on blind arcading.

The Buck brothers' view of Tattershall

The Tower on the Moor

TORKSEY CASTLE   SK 836788

Leland mentions a castle at Torksey, but the existing impressive ruin on the east bank of the River Trent is the west range of a mansion built by Sir Robert Jermyn probably in the 1560s. Above a lofty lower storey of stone it has two upper levels of brick. There are many mullioned windows, including a bay of ten lights in the northernmost of the four projecting turrets or bays, one of which contains a spiral staircase.

TOTHILL CASTLE   TF 420810

A low motte and a bailey to the SW lie by a marsh, west of the Great Eau stream.

TOWER ON THE MOOR

TF 211640

All that remains of a brick tower near Woodhall Spa built by Lord Cromwell in the mid 15th century is a polygonal stair turret 17m high which projected very boldly from one corner. No details of the main tower are known other than it had four storeys.

WELBOURN CASTLE SK 968544 V

This is a large and rather overgrown ringwork, the ditch of which probably contained water. A document of c1158 refers to Hugh de Bayeux granting land to Robert Rabaz in return for the construction of a perch of walling at this castle.

WELTON MOTTE TF 476698 V

A small mound lies by a bend of a track 1km NNE of Welton le Marsh Church. West of the mound and south of the track is a moated site.

WITHERN: CASTLE HILL TF 427822 V

This quadrangular platform with a wide dry moat lies at the west end of the village. The Fitzwilliam family later had a house in the moated site east of the church.

WRANGLE CASTLE TF 413531

King's Hill, 2.7km NNW of Wrangle church, is a low motte with a bailey and various outworks to contain former wet moats.

WYBERT'S CASTLE TF 335410

A stream runs past the west side of an oval enclosure 0.5km east of Wyberton Church, and probably once filled its moat. The site was occupied during the 12th and 13th centuries and possibly later.

OTHER POSSIBLE FORTIFIED SITES IN LINCOLNSHIRE

ASLACKBY TF 085305 Dubious earthwork immediately north of church.
BELLEAU TF 402784 Brick barn is much altered hall range of a moated house of the Lords Willoughby d'Eresby (see entry for Eresby).
BENNIWORTH Site unknown. Its constable is mentioned in 1216.
BOSTON Town had thin brick wall, more a customs barrier than a fortification.
CAISTOR TA 116012 Built by King Stephen in 1143, probably just west of church.
CASTLE DYKE TF 008143 Unimpressive remains of earthwork.
DALBY TF 412698 Possible motte.
FRISKNEY TF 451549, 450556, 463556, Three moated sites, one of which may mark the site of building licensed for crenellation in 1303.
GRANTHAM Possibly had a castle but no details of it are known.
KETTLETHORPE HALL SK 847756 - South and east arms of moat of house of the Swynford family. Gateway looks like 18th century folly built of old parts.
LANGWORTH TF 006752 Ponds mark site of bishop's palace mentioned 1336.
LEA SK 836881 or 843872 Moated sites, possible locations of embattled house.
REDBOURNE SK 974999 Castle Hills east of church has remains of two enclosures.
SPALDING TF 248231 Ivo Tallboys is thought to had a castle on or near this site.
SPILSBY TF 394652 Moat remains of possible fortified house.
THORNTON ABBEY TA 115190 The walled and moated precinct has a very large embattled gatehouse of stone and brick with octagonal turrets at the corners and on either side of the inner portal. One contains a stair and the others small rooms. Licensed by Richard II in 1382, the gatehouse contains two upper chambers, one a court room. Extending awkwardly askew in front of the gate is a 35m long 16th century barbican of brick with side loopholes and round turrets at the outer end.
WRAGBY TF 135777 Moats south of church may mark the site of a castle.

GAZETTEER OF NORTHAMPTONSHIRE CASTLES

ALDERTON MOTTE   SP 741470

Channel Four's Time Team investigated this almost triangular ringwork about 65m across in 2000, and found traces of a possible stone gatehouse. From the trench on this part of the site came a horse harness trapping probably of late 14th century date and suggesting the site remained in use until the early 15th century. Traces of a timber platform were found on the rampart. The manor was held by Robert de Mortain in the 1070s but the castle maybe an unlicensed mid 12th century fortress.

ASTWELL CASTLE   SP 608441

Thomas Lovett built himself a new moated house here after obtaining the manor by an exchange of lands. Originally called Astwell Manor, it has been called Astwell Castle since 1886. The moat has been filled in and all that remains of the buildings grouped around a small court is a three storey embattled gatehouse, about 8.5m by 7m on the east side. Flanking the entrance passage (now blocked) are a latrine turret on the south side and a porter's lodge on the north. Adjoining the latter is a stair turret on the west side. A short length of embattled walling adjoins the latrine turret. The hall lay in the west wing, with the main private apartments on the south, and a chapel at the east end, whilst the service rooms lay on the north. After the death of Thomas Levitt in 1586 the house passed by marriage to George Shirley of Staunton Harold, who demolished much of the old building and built a spacious new mansion with over forty rooms in 1606. Most of it was demolished in the late 18th century.

BARBY MOTTE   SP 543707

Hidden beyond a housing estate is an oval mound 1.5m high surrounded by a ditch.

The gatehouse at Astwell

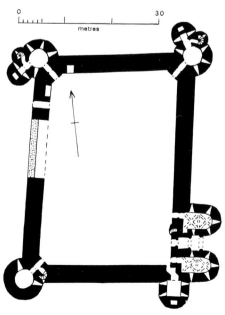

Plan of Barnwell Castle

Barnwell Castle

BARNWELL CASTLE   TL 049852

Berengar le Moyne handed over this castle to Peterborough Abbey in 1276, although he continued to inhabit it as a tenant. Earlier that year a jury reported that he had built the castle illegally (i.e. without a royal licence) ten years earlier. When the abbey was dissolved in 1539 the castle was purchased by Sir Edward Montagu, who built a new house in the outer court. This building, with considerable additions of the 1890s and 1913, now forms the residence of the Duke of Gloucester.

The castle ruins lie south of the house, and to the west, above the Barnwell Brook, are earthworks of an older castle probably built by the le Moyne family in the 1130s. The stone castle has a courtyard 40m by 27m surrounded by a curtain wall 3.6m thick and 9m high, which remains intact apart from its parapet and a 12m long breach in the west wall, now closed by a thin modern wall. At the SW, NW and NE corners are towers 8.5m in diameter in which are loops flanking the curtains, all three having entrances at ground level. The SW tower has a spiral stair next to its entrance passage and two square upper rooms with fireplaces and later mullioned windows. The other two towers have a unique trilobed plan, since they have projecting turrets 5.5m in diameter containing latrines on each of two storeys, and smaller staircase turrets project from one of the resulting re-entrant angles. There is a postern in the west wall close to the NW tower. At the SE corner there are adjoining each other a D-shaped tower facing south and a gatehouse with twin U-shaped towers facing east. The gateway passage has a double-chamfered outer portal with a portcullis groove and a tunnel vault. The gateway towers have rib-vaulted basements, each with five loops, and the basement of the other tower was also originally rib-vaulted. The doorways to the rooms are round-headed and single-chamfered. By the inner portal is a staircase to an upper room over the passage with large windows. From it there is access to the tower upper rooms. There seem to have been lean-to buildings against all the curtains. Reports of the castle being "late demolished" by the Duke of Montague in 1704 must refer to the destruction of these buildings, although it is possible that the gatehouse and towers, which are now of a uniform height with the curtains, then each lost an extra storey (unless these parts were never completed, which is not unlikely). There are no signs of a moat.

Barnwell Castle

BARTON SEAGRAVE CASTLE   SP 885769

Of the house which Nicholas Seagrave was licensed by Edward II to crenellate in 1310 there remains a moated platform 80m by 40m, the SW corner of which is recessed (or has been destroyed). A second moated platform about 35m square to the north is now interpreted as a garden feature or fishpond.

BENEFIELD CASTLE   SP 987885

In a private garden west of the churchyard is a platform surrounded by a ditch 2.5m deep with a counterscarp bank 1m high. In the early 18th century some walling still remained on the platform, although nothing now remains visible. King John permitted this site to be fortified in 1208. It is referred to as "an old castle" in 1298, and was probably abandoned about that time.

BOUGHTON HOUSE   SP 900815

Richard Whetehille was licensed by Edward IV to crenellate his house here in 1473, and the building is said to have once had gunloops, although the hall and cross wings buried in the present house appear to be a few years later than the 1470s. The west wing has small 16th century mullioned windows towards the quadrangle known as Fish Court. The lawyer Sir Edward Montague (one of executors of Henry VIII's will) purchased the estate c1530 and his son extended the house. Further extensions, plus the hall ceiling, and the fine French-style north front were done for the first Duke of Montague, who inherited the estate in 1683.

BRACKLEY CASTLE   SP 581363

There are only very slight remains of the castle here destroyed by Henry II in 1173. It stands at the southern edge of the town and has a barn on top of it.

BRADDEN MANOR   SP 648487

A building dated 1819 but actually of several old periods stands on the site of a manor house for the crenellation of which John Holcot obtained a licence from Edward IV in 1477.

Earthworks at Braybrooke

BRAYBROOKE CASTLE SP 779845 V

A platform 60m by 50m surrounded by a 2m deep ditch 15m wide lies within a trepezoidal outer platform, west of which is another enclosure with a small platform isolated in its NE corner. A lake lay to the north of the site. Edward I licensed Thomas Latimer to fortify this site in 1304 and it was described as a castle in 1361.

CASTLE ASHBY SP 863592 O

In 1306 Walter Langton, Bishop of Lichfield, obtained a licence from Edward I to crenellate his house here, he having recently obtained the manor from the Earl of Huntingdon. The descendants of Bishop Langton's sister sold the manor in 1423 to Lord de Grey. He already had a seat nearby at Yardley Hastings (where a solar block of an unfortified house of c1320-40 still remains) and seems to have dismantled the castle at Ashby. In the 1530s Leland described it as "clene down, and is made a septum for beasts". Back in 1512 both Ashby and Yardley Hastings, plus several other neighbouring manors, had been purchased by Sir William Compton. The present house, probably on the same site as the castle, was begin in 1574, and was probably completed in time for Queen Elizabeth's visit in 1600.

CRANSLEY MOTTE SP 825767

A 5m high mound in woodland NW of the church has had a deep trench cut into it.

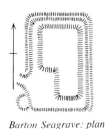

Barton Seagrave: plan

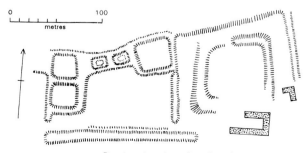

Braybrooke: plan of earthworks

CULWORTH CASTLE   SP 545470   V

North of the church is a ringwork about 40m by 33m enclosed by a ditch except on the SE, where the rectory garden intrudes upon the earthworks.

DAVENTRY CASTLE   SP 581612

The John of Gaunt Hotel stands on the site of a house once owned by its namesake. It had a square walled court with a double ditch and a gateway facing SE and two other towers. Much of the site was quarried away in the 19th century but a small portion of the ditch remains. To the east (at SP 858612)lies Burnt Walls, a very large triangular enclosure with a rampart 2m high and a 2m deep ditch.

DRAYTON HOUSE   SP 963800

The rib-vaulted cellar with octagonal piers of the former solar block NE of the medieval hall goes back to 1328, when Simon de Drayton obtained a licence to crenellate the house from Edward III, or possibly even earlier. The hall then lay between NW and SE courts, and had a porch facing the principal approach through the NW court, which is now only enclosed on two sides. The SE court still has a far end wall 1.6m thick, strengthened with four buttresses (originally there was a fifth to the SW) and having an embattled parapet with cross-loops in the merlons. A turret was added to the NE side of the solar block in the late 15th by Henry Greene, his namesake ancestor having purchased the house in 1361. The long NE wing flanking both courtyards and having irregularly distributed mullion-and-transom windows is dated 1584 and was added by Lord Mordaunt of Turvey. The wing ends in towers at either end and contains a secret hiding place above the State Bedroom, Lord Mordaunt being a Catholic who ended his days a prisoner in the Tower of London after being implicated in the Gunpowder Plot. He also widened the hall block by adding new parts on either side of the porch, and also the SW wing of the SE court, now facing towards a small service court.

In the 1670s new ranges were built around three sides of the SE court, a new central gateway was provided, and a stableblock on the SW side of a new forecourt. After the Earl of Peterborough (last of the Mordaunt male line) died in 1697, Drayton passed to his daughter, then married to the Duke of Norfolk. She lived at Drayton with her lover Sir John Germaine, who in 1701 became her second husband. In 1702 they employed William Talman to rebuild the kitchen and service rooms SW of the hall, which was itself mostly rebuilt. The NE and SW ends of the surviving courtyard have colonades of Roman Doric columns on which are the arms of Sir John Germaine and his second wife Betty, a daughter of the Earl of Berkeley, who long outlived him.

Drayton House

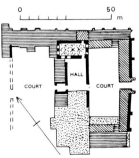

Plan of Drayton House

EARLS BARTON CASTLE   SP 852638   F

The church lies on a promontory used as the bailey of a low motte added on the north side. The motte or Berry Mount) has a ditch 4m deep on the north side but has been later partly cut away on its south side. The motte was overlooked by the fine Saxon tower of the church which the Norman lord probably intended to dismantle, so the castle was probably short-lived.

EASTON NESTON HOUSE   SP 702494

The existing mansion of the 1680s and early 1700s built for Sir William Fermor, later Lord Lempster, lies on the site of an older house, for the crenellation of which Richard Empson obtained a licence from Henry VII in 1499.

Fotheringhay: last remnant of keep

FARTHINGSTONE: CASTLE DYKES   SP 618566

This tree-clad earthwork has a ringwork 40m in diameter and with a 2m high bank full of rubble, probably from a collapsed curtain wall. It lies on the south side of an enclosure 180m long by 80m wide which is protected by a rampart and ditch and seems to have been divided into two baileys. On the SE is a double rampart system. An entrance causeway faces a D-shaped outer bailey 130m across lying to the north.

FOTHERINGHAY CASTLE   TL 062930   F

Simon de St Liz, Earl of Huntingdon and Northampton, is assumed to have founded this castle at the end of the 11th century, although the first mention of it is 1212, when King John ordered David, Earl of Huntingdon to surrender it, although it appears that it was not handed over until 1215. The castle was briefly occupied by the rebellious William de Forz in 1221, and it was attacked unsuccessfully in 1264 by Robert de Ferrers, Earl of Derby. It was owned during this period by the Balliols, but was forfeited in 1294, when John Balliol, King of Scotland, defied Edward I. During Richard II's reign the castle was rebuilt by his uncle, Edmund Langley, Duke of York. He intended to found a college within the castle bailey, as Windsor and Warkworth at about the same period, but in the event the college founded in 1411 by his son at at the parish church, which was rebuilt on a grand scale. There is a mention of chambers, latrines, turrets and a kitchen in the 1460s, when Edward IV was having work done upon them. He had granted the castle to his mother Cecily, Duchess of York, but recovered it by an exchange of lands. Mary, Queen of Scots was held prisoner in the castle keep from 1586 until her trial and execution in the 21m long aisled hall in February 1587. The castle was dismantled in the 1630s.

Beside the north bank of the River Nene lies an oval motte 7m high with a summit 33m by 27m which once bore a horse-shoe shaped shell-wall, the "kepe very anncient and strong" probably built in the 14th century, the only relic of which is the fallen chunk of masonry lying at the foot of the mound. The "fair lodgyns" Leland also mentions may have been within the shell wall or down in the bailey platform 58m by 45m to the east. A ditch up to 4m deep surrounds the motte and bailey. A causeway on the north marks the entrance. To the SE lies an outer bailey defined by a ditch and there are traces of a third bailey where Castle Farm now lies.

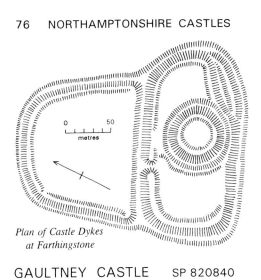

Plan of Castle Dykes
at Farthingstone

Reset postern at Northampton

GAULTNEY CASTLE   SP 820840

In 1140 Alan of Brittany captured William de Albini's castle of Gaultney or Galclint. Alan was subsequently captured by Rannulf, Earl of Chester, and starved until he was persuaded to order the castle to be surrendered. The grid reference given is only approximate and lies in an area now completely altered by opencast mining.

HARRINGWORTH MANOR   SP 917975

East of the church and south of the River Welland lies a manor house with one 14th century two-light window and a later range behind. William, Lord Zouch was licensed by Richard II in 1387 to crenellate his house here, and a later Lord Zouch was granted another crenellation licence by the young Henry VI in 1431. John Leland refers to the building as a castle in the 1530s.

HIGHAM FERRERS CASTLE   SP 961688

The only remains of a stone castle of three wards are a small pond in White Close which may represent part of the northern moat, and slight traces of a possible rampart in the northern part of the churchyard. The manor belonged to the Peverels in the 12th century, and later passed to the Ferrers family. It became part of the earldom of Lancaster in 1266 and thus became royal when Henry IV took the throne in 1399. There was only a capital messuage here in 1298, and the first mention of a castle is in 1322, which would make Thomas, Earl of Lancaster the likely builder. The castle was kept in repair during the 15th century and the hall was rebuilt at a cost of £368 in 1411-13 after a fire. The hall was then embattled and had a porch with a chamber above it. The kitchen was remodelled in preparation for a visit by Edward IV in 1462. Henry VII allowed the castle to decay and in 1523 Henry VIII allowed Sir Richard Wingfield to remove stone from it to rebuild Kimbolton Castle.

HYMEL CASTLE   SP 972977   V

Most of the house which replaced the Augustinian Abbey of Finshade in the 18th century was itself demolished in 1956. Surrounding it, and most obvious on the SW side, are the 2.5m high ramparts of the castle of Hely or Hymel which stood on this site when it passed to the Augustinians on the death of Robert de Engaine in 1208.

The earthworks at Long Buckby

LILBOURNE CASTLE   SP 561775   F

Near the church, just south of where the River Avon forms the boundary between Northamptonshire and Leicestershire is a motte rising 7m to a summit 9m across with a D-shaped bailey to the NE 49m in diameter with a 2m deep ditch. The 45m square SE bailey with a rampart up to 5m high with raised corners probably for timber towers is thought to be an addition of the 1140s by Gerard de Camville. There is a counterscarp around the SW and SE sides. At Hill Ground, to the SW at SP 553771, is a second motte rising 7.5m from a ditch 2m deep to a summit 15m across.

LITTLE HOUGHTON CASTLE   SP 806606

On the south side of the River Nene 1km north of Little Houghton church is the 15m high Clifford's Hill motte rising 15m from a 5m deep ditch to an oval summit 30m by 22m. There are slight traces of a probable ringwork to the SW at SP 803597.

LONG BUCKBY CASTLE   SP 625675   F

The ringwork is 4m high with a ditch 2m deep. Little remains of a bailey to the west, but excavations in the 1950s showed that it had a 12th century curtain wall and at least one internal building of stone. A castle here is mentioned in King John's reign.

MOOR END CASTLE   SP 753446   V

Only a moated platform and fishponds remain of the fortified house which Edward III licensed Thomas de Ferrers to crenellate in 1347. The building had passed to Thomas le Despenser by 1363 when the king took possession of it, and had a stone-walled court with a gatehouse and corner towers, traces of which were found in the 19th century. Between 1363 and 1365 the king visited Moor End several times and spent £860 on reroofing the hall, building a new royal chamber and a chapel with painted glass windows, providing a corridor between the old and new chambers, remodelling the gatehouse, and providing the rooms in the towers with fireplaces. Later in the 1360s there are several other references to work at the castle, including a new padlock for the main gate "after the escape of prisoners there". Moor End was later held in dower by each of Richard II and Henry IV's queen consorts, and then was held by Humphrey, Duke of Gloucester, uncle of Henry VI.

MOULTON CASTLE

Moulton is said to have had a stone castle, with a motte, but its location is uncertain.

NORTHAMPTON CASTLE   SP 748605

The castle said to have been built by Simon de Senlis as the caput of his earldom of Northampton passed to the Crown upon his death c1111. Excavations in 1961 have shown that the castle took the place of several Saxon houses and that it had a small motte later absorbed into the rampart of the inner bailey. The bailey rampart was then 24m wide and 6m high and was fronted by a formidable ditch 27m wide and 9m deep. The castle had extensive water-filled moats and was enlarged by Henry I, the monks of St Andrew's priory being compensated for land taken for this purpose. The town also seems to have first been fortified during this period. Simon de Senlis II recovered the castle on King Stephen's accession in 1135 and held it until his death in 1153. Henry II subsequently claimed the castle and it was then retained as a royal stronghold. Here he fell out with his Archbishop of Canterbury, Thomas Becket, accusing Becket of misusing funds he had handled as Chancellor. The keep and other parts of the castle were repaired during the rebellion of 1173-4, and £107 was spent upon the keep in 1181-3, and further sums under Richard I in 1192-3. King John is known to have spent about £300 upon the castle. Early in 1215 it was garrisoned and provisioned and in April withstood an attack by the barons. There was a more serious attack upon it later in the year by a rebel force equipped with French siege engines, but King John brought an army up to relieve it.

Over £300 was spent on repairs after the sieges of 1215 and there is mention of a tower named after Faulkes de Breaute, who was constable from 1216 until his rebellion in 1223. Improvements to the chapel are mentioned in 1236 and 1244. During this period the apartments for the queen were refurbished and a chapel for her own use was added. It was glazed and wainscoted in 1248-9, and at the same time the palisade of the outer bailey was repaired. Repairs to the curtain wall of the inner bailey and its towers were authorised in 1251-2. In 1258-9 the gaol was repaired following a report that it was incapable of keeping prisoners secure. The west curtain wall was in a very serious state of decay, and it was only rebuilt after it finally collapsed into the River Nene in 1266. Two years previously the kings's forces had occupied the town and castle, then held by Simon de Montfort, Earl of Leicester, without serious resistance because of the decayed and incomplete condition of their defences. The last remnant of the castle, a length of heavily buttressed walling destroyed in 1879 when the railway station goods shed was built across the middle of the inner bailey, was probably that which replaced the fallen wall.

The domestic buildings at Rockingham

Further repairs were done for Edward I in 1280-1 and 1287-8, and the town defences were also then improved. A new chamber with a wardrobe and chimney were erected for the king and queen in 1301. Edward I's younger sons Thomas and Edmund were living in the castle in 1306 and that occasioned further repairs. The castle seems to have ceased to serve as a royal residence after 1318, when the hall, the great chamber, "the long chamber adjoining the hall on the south" and "the lower chapel towards the south" were all destroyed by fire. Their rebuilding costs were estimated at £702 in 1323, when a survey mentions the "new tower", six other small towers, the new gate, two old gates, the barbican, the "mantellum" or curtain wall, the hall court and a garden. In 1329 the great hall was renovated at a cost of £57 to serve for the holding of law courts. It may be significant that when a parliament was held at Northampton in 1380, the young Richard II stayed at Moulton, probably because the castle buildings were unfit to accommodate him. A new prison was erected in 1385-6. These two buildings were kept in repair when everything else was allowed to decay, and the defences were described as ruinous in 1593. Charles II had the town walls demolished in 1663 since the town had been a Parliamentary stronghold during the Civil War, and parts of the castle were also then dismantled, a new sessions house for law courts being built elsewhere in the town. The provision of a new bastion in front of the castle gateway during the 1640s proves it was then still defensible. In the 18th century both baileys were in use as orchards.

Parts of the remaining earthworks were levelled in the 1820s and the construction of the new railway station in the 1880s saw the destruction of everything else, except a postern from the west wall reset in the southern boundary wall of the goods yard. This postern now stands in a wall facing Marefair. Until the 1880s there survived a flat topped mound which is assumed to have been the site of the keep. A skeleton was found under it in 1827. The layout of the west and south walls of the large (3.5 acres) bailey were recorded before destruction and the location is known of walls of internal buildings, a D-shaped tower on the south side, four wells, and a vaulted chamber discovered just west of St Andrews Road in 1863. The main north-facing gatehouse lay where this road traversed the bailey, one jamb of the passageway being revealed in 1883. There was a second gateway on the SE side, east of where the road crosses the site. Traces of the bailey moat remain in the grounds of a rectory off Fitzroy Street on the NE side. See page 76.

PRESTON CAPES CASTLE   SP 576549

A bailey (now the site of a farm) probably once defended the southern side of a 4m high ringwork about 27m in diameter with a strong counterscarp bank on the descending ground to the north, where there are other outworks. Hugh de Leycestre founded a priory near his castle here c1090, but the monks soon moved to Daventry.

Walker's House and gatehouse inner front at Rockingham

ROCKINGHAM CASTLE   SP 867913   O

In Domesday Book it is recorded that the manor "was waste when King William ordered a castle to be made". Either William II (1087-1100) or his brother Henry I (1100-35) probably built the keep and curtain wall. Minor repairs by Henry II are recorded in 1187-08. King John visited the castle fourteen times between 1204 and 1216, and spent nearly £200 upon it, including building a new tower. The castle suffered some damage in 1220, when it was besieged and captured from William de Forz by Hubert de Burgh on behalf of the young Henry III, and it seems to have remained in that state until repaired in the 1250s. The gatehouse was added by Edward I, who remodelled the domestic buildings and added a NW tower. Edward III granted the castle to his queen and used it occasionally. The castle was subsequently allowed to decay and it was described by Leland c1540 as "faullith to ruine".

In 1553 Edward Watson leased the castle from the Crown and began restoration. He divided up the great hall and inserted a ceiling which is dated 1579. His son entertained James I at the castle in 1603. The long gallery contains a fireplace dated 1634 which marks the time of its completion by Sir Lewis Watson after a long delay since it had been begun by his father. It was shortened after the Civil War, during which the castle was occupied by the Parliamentarians, withstood several Royalist attacks, and then was demilitarised by the destruction of the keep and most of the curtain wall. Although censored by the king for losing the castle, Sir Lewis was forgiven and made a baron in 1644. The 3rd baron was made Earl of Rockingham but the title died with his grandsons, when the castle passed to Lewis Monson, who took the name Watson and became Lord Sondes. He and his son only used the castle occasionally but in 1836 Richard Watson, the youngest brother of the 3rd Lord Sondes, took up permanent residence at Rockingham. The castle eventually passed to his daughter's son Sir Michael Culme-Seymour. His son has now handed it over to a nephew, Michael Saunders, who has added to his own the Watson surname.

The gatehouse at Rockingham

William I's castle consisted of a central motte with a D-shaped inner bailey 140m long by 100m wide to the north on the end of a promontory, and an outer bailey about 120m square to the SE, which was never stone walled. The large but low motte eventually bore a spacious shell keep with lodgings inside it. Cannon were mounted upon it during the Civil War, after which most of it was destroyed along with much of the mound itself, but the lower part of the section of the shell wall facing the bailey remains in a lowered and partly refaced condition as a garden terrace. The rest has been replaced by a circular formal garden. In 1250 the keep was in a badly cracked condition, and then contained six chambers on the same level. Leland mentions the barbican of the keep, a part of which was revealed by excavation in 1935 and remains visible to the SE.

The bailey is effectively divided into an eastern part in which lie the domestic buildings, and a western part, now gardens enclosed by low retaining walls which are curved inwards at two corners thought to have had large 13th century circular towers. Apart from one short section remodelled as garden lookout on the eastern motte slope, the curtain wall only remains on the east side. Herringbone masonry visible inside a room suggests an early date for it. Towards the north end of this side lies the gatehouse of the 1270s, a scaled-down version of others of the same period in Wales (see plan on page 82). It has D-shaped towers containing outer rooms flanking an arch with a portcullis groove. The passage itself is flanked by rectangular inner rooms, that on the south having a latrine and a blocked doorway towards a former staircase in a corner turret. The towers have cross-loops with bottom roundels, and there are others in the curtain and in a small square tower closer to the motte. The battlements are mid 19th century and it is likely that there was a third storey prior to the Civil War slighting. Extending from the gatehouse to the NE corner is the mid 16th century Walker's House, with a fine staircase of 1655, when it became the steward's lodging.

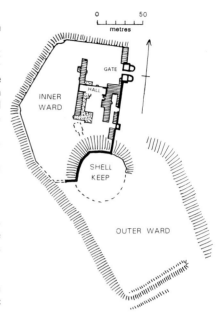

Plan of Rockingham Castle

Hall doorway at Rockingham

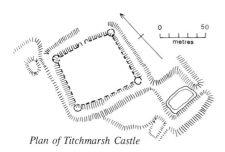

Plan of Titchmarsh Castle

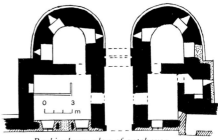

Rockingham: plan of gatehouse

SW of the gatehouse is the hall, extending from east to west and retaining two 13th century doorways, that on the north having roll-mouldings with keels and fillets. In the Panel Room to the west (which was originally part of the medieval hall) are parts of two tall shafted windows and a 14th century window which possibly served a gallery. The panelling itself is of the 1680s. South of the hall is a court and also a narrow alleyway between buildings, known as the Street. The laundry at the south end of the Street is dated 1669. The buildings east of the hall date from the 1580s, and extending north and south from its west end are long ranges of the 1570s, although the southern part was remodelled c1670. The square tower east of the south range, and the polygonal tower projecting west from the north range were added in the mid 19th century to designs by Anthony Salvin. He also added a staircase projection on the north side of the hall. Various modifications to the buildings, and a rebuilding of all the roofs, was undertaken in the 1960s.

SIBBERTOFT: CASTLE YARD   SP 690832

On the end of a spur overlooking the junction of two streams to the north is a motte rising 4m above a ditch dividing it from a kidney-shaped bailey 100m by 15m on the more level ground to the south. The motte summit measures about 15m by 11m.

SULGRAVE CASTLE   SP 556453   V

Excavations in the 1960s on the 4m high ringwork 37m by 32m lying west of the churchyard found evidence of a drystone tower in the rampart and that the site had previously been occupied by a Saxon timber hall on stone footings which was rebuilt in the 11th century. The ditch has been obliterated on the SW side.

THORPE WATERVILLE   TL 022814   V

Edward I licensed Walter Langton, Bishop of Lichfield to crenellate his house here in 1301. Edward II confiscated the manor and gave it to Aymer de Valence, Earl of Pembroke. It passed to the Hollands and then to John, Lord Lovell, and in 1461 was captured by a Yorkist force equipped with cannon, after which it was given to the Duchess of Exeter. Henry VII gave the house to his mother, the Countess of Richmond, and in 1557 it was given to Sir William Cecil. The moats have been mostly filled in but there remains a large barn converted from the hall with two circular windows high up, and the farmhouse contains a reset lancet window.

THRAPSTON CASTLE   SP 996787

Modern bungalows west of Chancery Lane lie upon the lowered mound, which originally had a wide ditch and possibly a stone building on top.

The earthworks at Titchmarsh

TITCHMARSH CASTLE   TL 024795

In 1304 John, Lord Lovell was licensed by Edward to crenellate his castle at Titchmarsh. Only a platform 65m by 58m surrounded by a dry moat 15m wide with a pond beyond the SE corner now remains but excavations in the late 19th century revealed evidence of a thin curtain wall forming a revetment to the platform and having hexagonal towers up to 8m in diameter projecting from it into the moat at the corners. This building seems to have replaced an older stone-built castle which had a rather smaller oval court and a complex of buildings within it, some of which may have survived the later expansion of the defended area. The building was described in 1347 as "a capital messuage enclosed like a castle with water and a stone wall". Another reference in 1367 suggest it was already then in decay.

TOWCESTER CASTLE   SP 693488   V

The town was provided with a stone-faced earth rampart by Edward the Elder in 917 as a defence against the Danes. It had previously been fortified by the Romans and a traces of the rampart remain behind the police station. On the NE side of the town is a 7m high motte called Bury Mount. Moat Lane takes the place of part of the water-filled ditch. There was probably a bailey to the south.

WEEDON LOIS   SP 602470   F

On the village green are slight tree-covered remains of a ringwork 3m high.

WOLLASTON MOTTE   SP 908629

From the High Street a path between houses leads up past the museum to a mound called Beacon Hill which rises 5m to a summit 20m across, on which a windmill was erected in the 13th century. There are traces of a ditch on the south side.

GAZETTEER OF CASTLES IN NOTTINGHAMSHIRE

ANNESLEY CASTLE   SK 509518

In 1220 the regents acting for the young Henry III ordered an enquiry into a stronghouse at Annesley in Sherwood Forest recently erected by Reginald Marc which was said to be built in such a fashion that it would be a nuisance to the neighbourhood. It is likely that the buildings were subsequently dismantled but still surviving are the probably earlier tree-covered earthworks of a bailey about 100m with a small motte (or buried stump of a tower) at the south end.

ASLOCKTON CASTLE   SK 743402   V

Cranmer's Mount on the east side of the village is a small motte with a rectangular bailey 25m by 35m east of it and another platform 25m by 30m beyond. The motte top was about 12m across but the eastern part seems to have been lowered.

ASPLEY HALL   SK 540414

Lenton Priory had a hunting lodge here in the form of a timber-framed hall with a 15th century brick tower with a spiral stair in a projecting SE corner turret. The tower measured about 7m square over walls up to 1m thick. It was incorporated into a new structure c1600 but was totally destroyed in 1968.

BEAUVALE PRIORY   SK 493490

The prior of the Carthusian monastery founded in 1343 by Nicholas de Cantilupe seems to have had as his lodging a three storey tower at the west end of the church. It had a gabled roof and a staircase in a projection connected the two upper rooms.

BOTHAMSALL CASTLE   SK 671732

This ringwork has a substantial rampart on the side most exposed to attack.

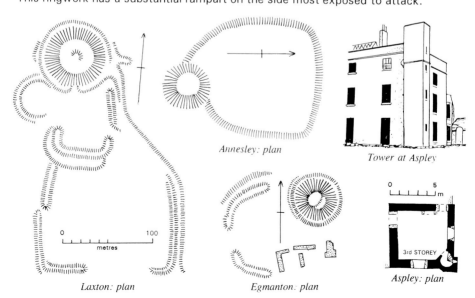

Annesley: plan

Tower at Aspley

Laxton: plan

Egmanton: plan

Aspley: plan

3rd STOREY

Egmanton Motte

CUCKNEY CASTLE   SK 566714

The churchyard partly overlies the slight remains of a castle erected by Thomas de Cuckney in King Stephen's reign. Henry II granted it to Stephen de Falconberg.

EGMANTON CASTLE   SK 735690   V

NW of the church is a motte called Gaddick Hill rising 6.5m above a 2.5m deep ditch to a summit 17m across, although the SE part is lower, possibly to accommodate games upon it on Shrove Tuesday. To the west are traces of the rampart and ditch of a bailey 90m across. Farm buildings obscure the SE part of the bailey.

GREASLEY CASTLE   SK 490470

Of the castle erected by Nicholas de Cantilupe under the terms of a licence granted by Edward III in 1340 there remain a length of walling 1.6m thick in a farm building and a large moated area with a fish pond in its SE corner. The walling formed part of the north side of a moated inner court 65m square lying on the north side of the site. At the NW corner is the blocked basement doorway of a round tower 6.5m in diameter. It is assumed the other corners had similar towers and that there were ranges on all four sides of the court. The gateway probably lay on the west and that the hall was on the east, where the base of a doorway was revealed by excavation in 1933. The Cantilupes inherited Greasley during King John's reign and under Henry III two of them were bishops of Worcester and Hereford. It later passed to the Zouch family and then was granted by Henry VII to the Savage family, but c1608 they sold it to Sir John Manners. The building seems to have been abandoned later in the 17th century, but there is nothing to link this with any events of the Civil War.

Greasley Castle

GRINGLEY CASTLE   SK 742908

Beach Hill is a pear-shaped mound 30m by 15m across on top, set on a promontory.

HALLOUGHTON TOWER   SK 690517   V

Across the road from the church is a small mid 14th century tower which formed a solar block of a residence of a prebend of Southwell Minster. The tower measures 7.5m by 5.2m and contained a basement lighted by two loops, a living room above with a fine two-light window with ogee-headed lights on the south side and a loop on the north, and a bedroom on top with more modest mullioned windows. The upper rooms are connected by a mural stair. Neither of them contains a fireplace. The tower has a gabled roof and there is no evidence that it ever had any wall-walks or parapets. The timber-framed hall adjoining the tower was rebuilt c1600, and then was encased in brick in the late 18th century, when another range was added.

KINGSHAUGH HOUSE   SK 765735

The ditch to the east of the house is a relic of the royal hunting lodge here which is mentioned as a castle in 1193, when it was held for Prince John against King Richard In 1210 John, by then king himself, spent £600 on building a new house here.

KIRKBY IN ASHFIELD   SK 491558

South of the church is a rectangular enclosure of uncertain date or purpose known as Castle Hill Camp. A U-shaped enclosure lies east of it.

Halloughton Tower

Halloughton Tower

Laxton Castle

LAXTON CASTLE   SK 720676   F

Stonework is visible on the south side of the 65m square inner bailey, in front of which is a ditch. At the north end, commanding a valley beyond, is a low motte 30m across on top, with a smaller mound in the centre, possibly the base of a tower. West of the bailey is a circular platform 30m across. It looks like a possible barbican although the main entrance is likely to have been through the 150m wide outer bailey to the south. The castle was built by the Alselin family and later passed to the de Everinghams, whose 14th century effigies lie in the church further south.

LINBY HALL   SK 534512

The south end of what looks like a three storey 17th century house is actually a medieval tower house about 9m square over walls from 1m to 1.5 thick. The original pointed-headed and chamfered doorway survives, probably 14th century, with its drawbar hole. The spiral stair in one corner is 17th century.

LOWDHAM CASTLE   SK 664468

Excavation of the motte here suggested it was occupied until c1400. It originally had a water-filled ditch.

Gatehouse at Newark

Gatehouse at Newark

NEWARK CASTLE   SK 796541   F

Newark became a possession of the bishops of Lincoln shortly after the Norman Conquest and excavations have shown that the fine stone castle built in the 1130s by Bishop Alexander replaced an older fortress of earth and wood. The bishop was allowed by Henry I to transfer the quota of knights for castle-guard which he owed at Lincoln to his new castle at Newark. In 1139 the castle, then described as magnificent and of ornate construction, was confiscated by King Stephen since Bishop Alexander was a supporter of Stephen's rival, the Empress Matilda. Although the castle remained a possession of the bishops until the 16th century it was often in the hands of the Crown. Henry II had possession of it between the death of Bishop Robert de Chesney in 1167 and his appointment of his illegitimate son Geoffrey Plantagenet as bishop in 1173. Newark was a favourite haunt of King John, who mistrusted the bishop and often held the castle in his own hands. During a visit in 1215 he ordered brattices to be made for it, probably palisades for a former outer ward to the north. In the summer of 1216 John ordered the castle to be handed back to the bishop, since he was in need of episcopal support now that many of the barons were in rebellion against him. For some reason the bishop refused to take it back, and John then ordered the castle to be destroyed. However, a few days later the king changed his mind and placed the castle in the custody of a mercenary captain named Robert de Gaugy. In October that year King John died in the castle after losing his treasure whilst crossing the Wash. The young Henry III soon ordered the castle to be handed back to the bishop but de Gaugy refused and was only forced to submit in 1218 after a siege by William Marshal, Earl of Pembroke, who then went on to win a battle at Lincoln. The castle was captured again in 1221 by William de Forz, Count of Aumale, in his short-lived rebellion against the young Henry III.

Site of great hall at Newark

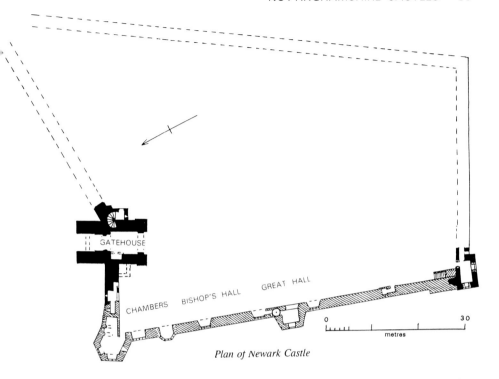

GATEHOUSE

CHAMBERS   BISHOP'S HALL   GREAT HALL

0   30

metres

Plan of Newark Castle

The west wall facing the river and the polygonal towers midway along it and at the NW corner represent a remodelling of the castle either by Bishop Sutton, (1280-1300) or Bishop Dalderby (1300-20), in an attempt to outdo the Bishop of Durham's new castle at Somerton (see page 60). In the 1470s Bishop Rotherham heightened and shortened his audience hall and added a fine oriel window over the river. The castle was resigned to the Crown by Bishop Henry Holbeach in 1547. It was leased to Sir Francis Leeke in 1560 and then to the Earl of Rutland in 1581 but was in a ruinous condition when the latter died in 1587. One of the trustees of the earl's will, Sir William Cecil then had the building repaired and improved, and in 1588 his son married Lady Elizabeth Manners in the castle chapel, and thus obtained possession of it. Newark was captured by Royalist cavalry in December 1643 and remained a Royalist stronghold (and mint) until King Charles finally ordered Lord Bellasis to surrender it in May 1646. A Parliamentary force under Sir John Meldrum which besieged it in 1644 was driven off by Prince Rupert. The final siege of the town and castle by a combined force of Parliamentarians and Scottish Presbyterians had lasted all through the winter since November 1645. Demolition of the defences began at once and the parish registers of North Collingham record the death of labourer Richard Thorneton in July 1646 "killed with the fall of stone at the pulling down of Newark Castle". However the NW tower and gatehouse were later re-occupied by squatters whilst the space outside the west wall became a coal wharf. By the late 18th century all traces of the eastern walls and ditch had vanished and the southern part of the side was a bowling green, whilst the northern part became tenements which were demolished in 1839 to make way for a cattle market. The ruin was partly restored in the 1840s and further work was done in the 1880s after the Corporation purchased the site from the Crown and landscaped the grounds as a public park.

Window in gatehouse at Newark

The SW tower at Newark   *Newark: gatehouse plan*

At the NW corner the ashlar-faced west front of the 1290s projects 8m further west than the original wall. This front is 73m long internally and the southern half still has its parapet, the wall-walk being 10.5m above the present internal level, and 18m above the ground outside, itself 2m above the river. The rest of the castle probably had a ditch deep enough to be filled with water from the river. Only the battered base remains of the 3m thick south wall. East of the gatehouse on the north side the 3.2m thick north curtain wall bent outwards so that the NE corner formed a sharp salient flanking the approach to the gateway. This irregularity of layout is thought to have been a legacy of a motte in the NE corner removed prior to the rebuilding of the 1130s. It resulted in the east side of the castle, now completely vanished, being about 100m long. It is assumed that the acute NE corner had a tower, from at least the 1290s, if not earlier, but there is no evidence for a tower at the SE corner.

The castle of the 1130s had thick walls but only minimal foundations and of it there remain only the SW tower and the gatehouse, together with short stubs of curtain walling each side of the gatehouse. A recent survey has shown that the curtain wall and gatehouse had timbers bonding them together, clear proof they were of one build. The SW tower rose 28m above the river to the top of its parapet and contained a prison at the original level of the courtyard, somewhat below the existing ground level, bedrooms with latrines on the second and third storeys, and a guard room reached from the wall-walk on the fourth storey. The second storey room was reached by a passage in the south curtain wall and the third storey by a staircase against the west curtain wall. The first three levels are all covered with barrel-vaults.

Amongst single-towered Norman gateways only the rather earlier example at Ludlow (later converted into a keep) can compare for magnificence with that at Newark, which measures 13.2m long by 9.3m wide and is ashlar faced on the outer side. The inner corners are clasped by wide pilaster buttresses, and there are smaller pilasters on the outer corners, which rise from a projecting base which has been refaced. The passageway was closed only by a two-leaved door but there must have been at least one drawbridge on the long wooden approach bridge over the moat, which was very wide at this point. A tiny guard room is squeezed into the west wall inside of where the gate lay. A staircase on the east side leads up to a room with an original window in the west wall which is thought to have been the bishop's audience chamber. A north doorway leads through to a thinly-walled and originally lean-to roofed chamber which had three wide windows overlooking the moat. By means of a timber gallery in the angle between this part and the curtain wall there was access to what may have been the bishop's bedchamber in a former turret on the west side of the gatehouse. It had a passage in the curtain wall to a latrine, the shute of which descended beside two others at a lower level in the original NW corner turret of the Norman castle. Over these other latrines was a spiral stair reached from an adjacent building giving access to another room over the supposed bishop's bedchamber. Later in the 12th century another room was created by heightening the northern adjunct, and in the 16th century all the rooms were given new windows and an upper room was created over the audience chamber, where an original circular window in the south wall was extended downwards. The timber gallery was made two storied and the latrine of the lower room in the west turret was replaced by a fireplace.

The windows either side of the semi-hexagonal middle tower, now lacking their mullions (although one retains seats) lighted a great hall, south of which lay service rooms with a chamber above, there being a two light window high up here, and a pair of latrines at courtyard level. Two more windows further north in the curtain wall lighted the bishop's private hall, and then there were two fine chambers in the NW corner, which used the older latrines in the north wall and had bedrooms leading off in the pentagonal NW corner tower. The lowest bedroom also has its own latrine. The inner walls of the hall and chambers may have been timber-framed. This suite of the 1290s superseded the more cramped layout of private rooms in the gatehouse. In the remodelling of the 1470s the northernmost of the two hall windows was replaced by a two storey oriel corbelled out from the wall and the lower and upper private chambers were given a four-light and six-light window respectively. The two windows high up further south represent a late 16th century remodelling in which a new floor was inserted to make new chambers in what had been the roof-spaces of the two halls, and the three-light window in the middle tower is also of that period. In the NW tower the floor levels were altered by 18th century squatters. Below the site of the bishop's hall is an undercroft divided by piers into groin-vaulted bays (two by four) divided by ribs. This cellar was reached by a stair (blocked in the 1490s) and had access to a round arched water gate with a slot for a draw-bar. The rectangular room under the lower chamber in the NW corner and the circular room in the base of the adjoining tower were either prisons or strong-rooms.

Excavations have shown that the lost town walls were early 14th century upon a partly stone revetted 12th century rampart. Traces of a water gate were found just west of the castle. The North Gate and the East Gate were destroyed in 1762 and 1784 respectively. There are, however, remains of the extensive system of earthwork fortifications built around Newark in the 1640s by both the Royalist defenders and the attacking Parliamentarian and Scottish forces. The best preserved and most accessible of several outlying forts is the Queen's Sconce to the SW (at SK 791531), a deeply ditched 50m square platform with four arrow-head-shaped corner bastions. The similarly-shaped King's Sconce (at SK 801548) was destroyed in the 1880s.

NOTTINGHAM CASTLE   SK 568395   O

The Danish stronghold at Nottingham, probably founded in 868, and captured and then repaired by Edward the Elder in 918, seems to have occupied the east end of the ridge above the River Trent. Nothing of significance remains of the town walls begun in the 1260s, and probably left incomplete in the 1330s. They ran along Park Row and Parliament street to join up with the castle on a high rock at the west end.

In 1068 William I ordered William Peveril to supervise the construction of a castle here. The Peverils remained constables and another William held the castle for King Stephen. The Earl of Gloucester burnt the town in 1140 but failed to take the castle, but it fell to the Empress Matilda after both King Stephen and William Peveril were captured at the battle of Lincoln in 1141. William recovered the castle, supposedly by scaling the rock, and held it until 1155 when Henry II accused him of conspiring to poison the Earl of Chester and his lands and honours were forfeited. Between 1170 and 1186 the king spent £1800 on providing both the upper and middle baileys with stone walls and new buildings. A tower, or small keep, is mentioned 1187-8.

When Richard I granted the former Peveril estates to his brother Prince John he excluded the castle at Nottingham, but John managed to obtain it anyway. After Richard finally returned to England in 1194 he was forced to besiege the castle, personally leading the assault on the outer bailey. Those captured within it were hung in view of the remaining defenders of the other two baileys, who were excommunicated by the Archbishop of Canterbury. They eventually surrendered and in the subsequent Council held in the great hall King Richard banished his brother from England. After John became king in 1199 Nottingham was one of his favourite seats. In 1212 the outworks were strengthened and a new tower built in the upper bailey. In that year he ordered the hanging of 28 Welsh hostages from the battlements after their fathers rebelled against him.

Henry III spent considerable sums upon the buildings of Nottingham Castle. Apart from the great hall which Henry II had built in the middle bailey there were halls for each of the king and queen. They each had their own chapels in the upper bailey, where there was also a chapel of St Nicholas, whilst there was another chapel in the middle bailey and two other chapels nearby, one of them in the park. During a visit at Christmas in 1252 Henry ordered the outer bailey palisade to be replaced by a new stone wall with a twin-towered gatehouse. His son Edward I is said to have added the tower named after him south of the gatehouse and also the Black Tower at the NE corner of the middle bailey. The castle was occupied by Robert de Ferrers, Earl of Derby in 1264 but recovered by Henry III without a fight.

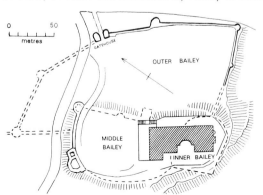

Plan of Nottingham Castle

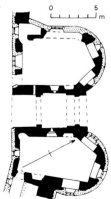

Nottingham: gatehouse plan

Outer gatehouse at Nottingham

During Edward II's reign there was considerable unrest in the area, the mayor being murdered in 1313 and the castle being besieged by the townsfolk for eight days in 1315. The king and queen often stayed in the castle at Christmas and in 1319 Queen Isabella sought refuge in it after narrowly avoiding being captured by a Scottish raiding party at York. In 1330 the widowed Queen Isabella and her lover Roger Mortimer, Earl of March were staying in the castle, prior to a holding of parliament at Nottingham, when supporters of the young Edward III entered the castle secretly at night, supposedly through the passage into the upper bailey from below known as Mortimer's Hole. Mortimer was arrested and taken off to London for trial and execution. Edward III rebuilt several of the upper bailey buildings and in 1348 provided his chapel there with six new windows of stained glass. In 1368 Edward ordered the constable, Stephen Romylow to rebuild the middle gate and erected a new kitchen in the middle bailey. Romylow also erected a new tower on the west side of the middle bailey and built a wall across the bailey from there to the gateway to close off the chambers occupying the southern part of the bailey. King David of Scotland was imprisoned in the castle in 1346.

Edward IV made his brother Richard, Duke of Gloucester his Lieutenant of the North, and the latter is assumed to have supervised the erection of the suite of two storey chambers with polygonal bay windows which lay on the north side of the middle bailey. During his short reign from 1483 until his defeat and death in 1485 Richard used the castle is his main residence. He added the large polygonal tower named after him which backed onto the apartments built during his brother's reign.

Strelley Hall: plan of tower

Gateway arch at Nottingham

The castle was said to be in a state of "dekay and ruyne" in 1525 but it was garrisoned during the Pilgrimage of Grace in 1536 and an inventory made after Henry VIII's death in 1547 noted as many as 45 tapestries in the apartments. Minor repairs were made before proposed (but cancelled) visits by Queen Elizabeth in 1562 and 1574, but the building was clearly in a poor condition by the early 17th century. Both James I and Charles I preferred to stay at the Duke of Clare's house, Thurland Hall, in Pelham Street during their frequent visits to Nottingham and after it was granted by James to the Earl of Rutland in 1623, considerable amounts of "timbre, lede and tyle" were plundered from it for building work elsewhere. In August 1642 the Civil War began when Charles I raised his standard on Derry Mount just outside the castle. However the castle soon fell to the Parliamentarians since the town supported them. Colonel Hutchinson found that the decayed buildings required much work to accommodate the four hundred strong garrison and their provisions. The Royalists managed to capture the town in January 1644, after making several other attempts at it, but the castle held out. It was finally abandoned and demolished with gunpowder in May 1651. William Cavendish, Duke of Newcastle obtained the site in 1674 and swept away what remained of the upper and middle bailey buildings for the construction of a palace. It was burnt by a mob during the Reform Bill riots of 1831 but was eventually restored in 1875-8 as a museum, a purpose it still serves.

The castle was one of the largest in medieval England and was generally regarded as one of the strongest. The upper bailey and part of the west side of the middle bailey stood above sheer rock-faces and the other sides were fairly well flanked. Very little remains of the buildings and defences of these two baileys but luckily a plan of them dated 1617 survives. The inner bailey built on the original motte (and called the motte in medieval records) had straight sides on the west and south meeting at an obtuse angle and a polygonal wall round the other sides, the enclosed area being about 52m by 45m. The 12m square tower on the north side seems to have formed a small keep and there were other towers about 10m square at the NW and SW corners and on the south side, and ranges of buildings between them, the entrance being beside the NW tower. The keep projected only very slightly outside the curtain and the other towers not at all. Under the south end of the fine classical style palace of 1675-9 occupying the now-reduced space of the upper bailey and the southern part of the middle bailey is Mortimer's Hole, probably the "postern giving access to the motte" built for Richard I in 1194-5, and supposedly the route used to enter the castle to effect the arrest of Roger Mortimer in 1330.

The D-shaped middle bailey was 65m wide and extended about 105m to the north. The square Romylow's Tower projected very slightly on the SW, and the square gatehouse projected very slightly from the east wall but had a barbican about 15m long in front of it which effectively flanked the whole of this side. From this gateway a set of steps alongside the curtain wall led southwards to the upper bailey. A D-shaped tower lay further north and the 11m diameter Black Tower at the NE corner, the base of which still exists. Also still remaining is the lower part of King Richard's Tower, a huge semi-octagonal structure 18m in diameter over walls nearly 4m thick, a larger version of a tower also attributed to Richard III at Sandal in Yorkshire. There were latrines in a projection where the curtain adjoined on the south side, and a square adjunct on the other side containing bedrooms. When the well in the tower basement was cleared out the finds included a cannon of c1500. The southern third of the middle bailey was filled with a complex of chambers. There were also chambers against the curtain between the gatehouse and the Black Tower and then from there the rooms added by Edward IV extended round the north side. Lying along almost in the middle of the bailey was the great hall built by Henry II in 1180 at a cost of £250. It had vanished by 1617, when Smithson's plan was drawn.

SE corner tower of outer bailey at Nottingham

Protecting the one approachable side of the castle was the outer bailey, which extended 100m east from the upper bailey east end and had a total length of 250m from the round tower at the SE tower to another tower at the acute NW corner, 55m beyond the middle bailey northern wall. The lower 6m of the southern half of the long eastern front, south of the gatehouse, together with the SE Tower, the 9m diameter Edward's Tower at a change of alignment of the curtain between these points, and a long section of the south wall with one small round turret still survive, although refaced. This lower part of the wall acted as a retaining wall on the inner side of the moat, and originally the wall stood 4 or 5m higher and the towers perhaps 10m higher than at present. The outer gatehouse is quite an impressive structure with tower 7.2m in diameter over walls 1.7m thick containing guard-rooms flanking a passageway 6m above the bottom of the moat, which is filled on the north side of the approach causeway. This causeway has one medieval arch with four chamfered ribs. Another arch of the 17th century takes the place of the former drawbridge. The passage was closed by a portcullis and, further in, a two-leaved doorway. All of the upper facing of the building dates from a restoration in 1908. Originally it must have been at least one full storey higher than its present height of 13m above the moat.

PERLETHORPE CASTLE

There is a mention of a castle at Perlethorpe in 1228. Its location is unknown.

SOUTHWELL MINSTER   SK 702538

The minster precinct withstood an attack in 1142. To the south are ruins of the outer walls with one corner tower of the eastern court of Archbishop Kemp of York's palace of the 1430s. His audience chamber remains intact beside the present palace on the site of the great hall. His private chambers lay in the east range upper storey.

STRELLEY HALL   SK 507421

In the hall SW corner is the barrel-vaulted basement of a 14th century tower 7.3m by 6.8m over walls up to 1.5m thick which probably existed by 1356, when Sir Sampson Strelley and his parishioners were allowed hold services in the chapel of his house for a year whilst the parish church immediately to the south was being rebuilt. The Strelleys were here by Henry I's reign, increased their estates by marriage with a Vavasour heiress c1280-90, and remained until the early 16th century. The buttressed sandstone walls of the outbuildings also predate the rebuilding of 1791.

WIVERTON HALL   SK 713363

The north side of the house of 1814 incorporates the lower storey of the gatehouse of the mansion of the Chaworth family (whose monuments are now at Langar). It was probably built by Sir Thomas in the 1440s or 50s, his mother Alice being the heiress of the Bret family, who had inherited Wiverton from the Heriz family in the late 13th century. The rest of the building was destroyed after capture by Parliamentary troops in 1645. A V-shaped battery of that period still remains in the fields SE of the house.

WORKSOP CASTLE   SK 593798

An irregularly shaped platform about 60m across remains in the angle between Norfolk Street and New Road. The castle is thought to have been founded by William de Lovetot in Henry I's reign. It may have been rebuilt in stone later since Leland suggests that stone from it was taken for the precinct wall of Worksop Priory.

BEAUMONT CASTLE   SK 850005

Castle Hill is a motte rising 11m to a summit 16m across. No bailey survives.

BURLEY CASTLE   SK 894120

By Alstoe farm is a damaged motte 4.5m high in the middle of a rectangular bailey, now only retaining a ditch on the NW. There are traces of several outer enclosures.

ESSENDINE CASTLE   TF 049128   V

The fine Norman church was once the castle chapel and its churchyard occupies the western half of a southern outer enclosure in front of a 4m high platform 57m by 45m surrounded by a ditch up to 30m wide which contained water. Beyond the southern enclosure are slight traces of fish ponds, and there was an additional triangular pond on the north side. In Henry II's reign William de Bussew married Rohesia, a descendant of Gilbert de Gaunt. The manor later passed to the earls of Warwick, reverted to Henry VIII, and then went to William Cecil. The terms of his will suggests there was then still a habitable house here, and amongst the titles granted by James I to his son Robert was that of Baron Cecil of Essendine.

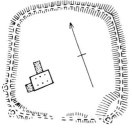

Oakham: site plan

LYDDINGTON PALACE   SK 895972   E

The Bede House north of the church is the chamber block at the SE end of the former hall of a palace of the bishops of Lincoln. Part of the SE wall may go back to the time of Hugh of Wells in the early 13th century. The NW wall and stair wing date from the time of Bishop Henry de Burghersh, who was licensed by Edward III in 1336 to crenellate the building. The precinct had a gatehouse but probably no moat as there was hardly enough space for one between the building and the church. No military features remain and the turret at the corner of the garden with a passage running through its base was purely ornamental. The block was remodelled by Bishop Russell in the late 15th century and again when converted into a hospital or almshouse in 1602 by Thomas, Lord Burghley. It is now administered by English Heritage.

Woodhead: plan

0   50
metres

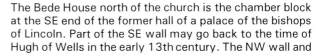

0   5
m

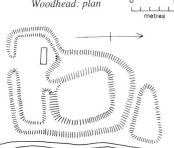

Plan of Essendine Castle

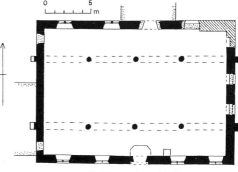

Oakham: plan of hall

Burley Castle

OAKHAM CASTLE   SK 862088   O

Oakham formed part of the dowry of the consorts of several of the Saxon kings of England. Edward the Confessor's widow Edith held it until her death in 1075 and only then did it revert to William I. He may have created the castle, perhaps on the site of a Saxon hall, although only a hall is referred to in Domesday Book. The size of the bailey, roughly a square of 115m, is what one would expect for a royal castle in a county town, although the motte in the SW corner is rather modest. The castle was surrounded by a wide wet moat and to the north lies a long, narrow outer enclosure known as Cutts Close. The hall was built by Walkelin de Ferrers in the 1180s, and the curtain wall around the bailey is probably early 13th century. The wall was over 2m thick and still partly stands up to 2m high, the bailey rampart being in fact mostly the collapsed and buried remains of it. A portion of the outer facing survives at the north end of the east side and the inner parts of round towers can be traced at the SW corner, not far north of that corner, and just west of the SE corner.

The castle is included in a list of castles required by the Crown for the general security of the country in 1308 and was well maintained in 1340 when a survey described the building as well walled, having a drawbridge with iron chains, and containing a "hall, four rooms, a chapel, a kitchen, two stables, a barn for hay, a house for prisoners", and "a room for the gate-keeper". It was then held by William de Bohun, Earl of Northampton. He and his son Humphrey were exceptions to the pattern of later medieval holders of the castle (none of whom probably used it as a residence) suffering violent deaths. Edward II's brother Edmund, Earl of Kent was executed in 1330, and Richard II's favourite Robert de Vere, Earl of Oxford was eventually driven out of the country by his enemies. Edmund, Earl of Rutland, a younger son of the Duke of York, was killed at Agincourt in 1415, Humphrey Stafford, Duke of Buckingham was killed at the battle of Northampton in 1459, his son was executed by Richard III and his grandson was executed by Henry VIII in 1521. Oakham then went to Thomas Cromwell, also eventually executed by Henry VIII, although his family held the castle until it was sold in the 1590s to Sir John Harrington. It was conveyed by his son to the Duke of Buckingam and then sold to the Earl of Nottingham, whose family held the castle until 1848.

The hall at Oakham

The hall at Oakham

The hall at Oakham remained in use as a court house long after the rest of the building fell into decay and is the best preserved example of its period. Noted also for its collection of horseshoes donated by visitors, it measures 19.8m by 13.4m within walls 0.9m thick and is divided by arcades of four round arches into a nave with lean-to aisles. The piers are circular and have finely carved crocket capitals, and there are hoodmoulds with dogtooth ornamentation over the arches. The respond corbels are animals in profile resting on pairs of human heads. The western part of the north aisle has polychrome interior masonry and two windows of two lights with solid tympana under a pointed outer arch. The windows are shafted and are ornamented with dog-tooth. These two windows correspond to the arcade arches. On the south side rebuilding has resulted in the doorway that originally opened onto the screens passage at the east end being moved to the middle of the wall, with two windows lying on either side of it. This doorway is round headed with nook-shafts with shaft-rings. The dormer windows on this side are not ancient, only one dormer (with a four-light mullioned window) being shown at the west end in a 17th century engraving. In the east wall are three blocked plain round-headed doorways to the service rooms (rebuilding has removed one jamb of the northern one). A few traces of these rooms were revealed by excavation in the 1950s, when a fine sculptured head of a man of c1250-75 was discovered in the moat. Over the service doorways is a 17th century mullioned window. Nothing remains of the chamber block at the west end, the rooms there, including two cells for prisoners, being no older than the 19th century.

PILTON MOTTE   SK 928023

This 3m high motte has a top diameter of 23m.

WOODHEAD CASTLE   SK 997116

A partly still wet-moated platform about 60m across with a rampart probably covering buried remains of buildings marks the site of the seat of the Grelley family, who obtained the manor c1150 from the Fitzwilliams. It passed to John de la Warre in the early 14th century and then went to the Brownes in the late 14th century.

A GLOSSARY OF TERMS

ASHLAR - Masonry of blocks with even faces and square edges. BAILEY - defensible court enclosed by a wall or a palisade and ditch. BARBICAN - Defensible court, passage or porch in front of an entrance. BASTION - A projection in front of but not rising above the outer wall of a fortress. CORBEL - A projecting bracket to support other stonework or a timber beam. CURTAIN WALL - A high enclosing wall around a bailey. FOREBUILDING - A fortified porch containing the entrance to a keep and sometimes also the stairs leading up to it. A chapel was often provided above. HERRINGBONE MASONRY - Stones laid diagonally in zig-zag courses. JAMB - A side of a doorway, window or other opening. KEEP - A citadel or ultimate strongpoint. The term is not medieval and such towers were then called donjons from which word is derived the work dungeon, meaning a strongroom or prison. LIGHT - A compartment of a window. LOOP - A small opening to admit light or air or for the discharge of missiles. MACHICOLATION - A slot for dropping or firing missiles at assailants. MOAT - A defensive ditch, water-filled or dry. MOTTE - A steep sided flat-topped mound, partly or wholly man-made. MULLION - A vertical member dividing the lights of a window. PARAPET - A wall for protection at any sudden drop. PILASTER BUTTRESS - A shallow buttress like a rectangular attached column. PLINTH - The projecting base of a wall. PORTCULLIS - A wooden gate (sometimes sheathed in iron) made to rise and fall in vertical grooves, being hoisted up by means of a windlass. POSTERN - A back entrance or lesser gateway. RINGWORK - An embanked enclosure of more modest size than a bailey, generally of greater width but less elevated than a motte summit. SCALE-AND-PLATT STAIRCASE - Staircase with short straight flights and turns at landings. SHELL KEEP - A small stone-walled court built upon a motte or ringwork. SOLAR - A private living room for the lord and his family. STRONGHOUSE - A mansion not fully equipped for a sustained defence against a proper siege but difficult to break into or burn down because of its solid walls and moat. WARD - A stone walled defensive enclosure.

PUBLIC ACCESS TO THE SITES   Codes used in the gazetteers.

E Buildings in the care of English Heritage to which an admission fee is payable.
F Ruins or earthworks to which there is free access at any reasonable time.
O Buildings opened to the public by private owners, local councils, trusts, etc.
V Buildings closely visible from public roads, paths, churchyards & open spaces.

FURTHER READING

Norman Castles in Britain, Derek Renn, 1968
Castellarium Anglicanum, D.Cathcart-King, 1983
A History of the King's Works, several vols, 1963-70
The Castles of England, Sir James D Mackenzie, two vols, 1897
Greater Medieval Houses of England and Wales, Vol II, Anthony Emery, 2000
The Victoria County Histories of Derby, Leics, Northants, Notts, Rutland.
Buildings of England Series mostly by N.Pevsner: volumes for Derbyshire,
   Leicestershire and Rutland, Lincolnshire, Northamptonshire, Nottinghamshire.
Pamphlet guides or monographs are available for: Ashby-de-la-Zouch, Belvoir,
   Bolsover, Castle Ashby, Grimsthorpe, Haddon, Kirby Muxloe, Lincoln, Newark,
   Nottingham, Peveril, Tattershall and Wingfield.
See also articles in the Archaeological Journal, Chateau Gaillard, Country Life,
   Fortress, Medieval Archaeology, and the annual transactions and journals of the
   various county archaeological societies and field clubs.